COUNTER INTUITIVITY

— Making meaningful innovation

Mario Van der Meulen

PUBLISHING

PUBLISHING

©2019 by Mario Van der Meulen.

All rights reserved. No part of this book may be reproduced, distributed or transmitted in any form or by any means, including photocopying, recording, or other electronic or mechanical methods, without the prior written permission from the publisher, except in the case of brief quotations embodied in critical reviews and certain other noncommercial uses permitted by copyright law. For permission requests, write to the publisher, addressed "Attention: Permissions Coordinator," at the web address below.

Mario Van der Meulen/MVDM Publishing
Publisher Registration No R2019041800006
Singapore SG 126843
mvdmpublishing.com or visit counterintuitivityprinciples.com

Book Formatting & Cover Layout Mario Van der Meulen

Cover Artwork ©Michael Cina - cinaart.com

Mario Van der Meulen can speak at your event or conference. For more information or to book participation to an event, contact the author at mvdmpublishing.com or linkedin/in/mariovdm

Counterintuitivity - making meaningful inovation
Mario Van der Meulen — 2019 1st ed.
ISBN 978-9-8114155-0-0

Contents

Prelude

Welcome – 1

Part 1 • The Matters Of Innovation

Human By Innovation – 14

The Thinking And Making Of Signs – 28

Unsuited For Uncertainty – 38

Now That The Earth Is No Longer Flat – 50

The Trees And The Forest – 66

Part 2 • Questioning The Questions

You Call That Innovation? – 82

Does One Size Fit All? – 92

Is It Only The Lucky Few? – 104

Is It Failure Or Incompetence? – 118

Do We Have To Collaborate? – 126

Part 3 • Acting On What Matters

Stop Digging Deeper Holes – 144

Inner Work Lives Matter – 156

It's About To Get Emotional – 176

Thinking Inside Out – 192

Part 4 • Creating Meaningful Innovation

The 9 Principles Of Counterintuitivity – 208

Do What Is Seemingly Unnecessary – 214

Make The Ordinary Unknown – 218

Choose More Boredom – 224

Create Moments Of Affinity – 232

Dare To Be A Little Ugly – 236

Forget How To Fear – 240

Change Is Permanent – 246

Decisions Just Are – 252

Remain Incomplete And Unfinished – 256

Creating Meaning Is A Design Task – 260

The Gift, Now Given – 268

Acknowledgements – 273

References – 275

Author's Bio – 279

For Kaeden,

The greatest adventure is what lies ahead

Today and tomorrow are yet to be said

The chances, the changes, they're all yours to make

The mould of life is in your hands to break

—J.R. Tolkien

a manifest of sorts

The role of innovators is to explore a future that by definition is uncertain, unpredictable, ever-changing.

If we continue the path of only thinking about the short term, the repeatable, the measurable, the known and the familiar, then we are no longer asking questions about our future.

The only outcome we will arrive at is an ever-narrowing mono-culture of frictionless efficiency. We will fall short of our own human potential; to shape a multi-culture of new possibilites by envisioning and creating that what is experienced as *meaningful*.

PRELUDE

Welcome

I HAVE WRITTEN a book. That only took twenty-five years of practicing and consulting design and with it, the most beautiful, difficult, disorienting yet meaningful experience of my life. The leap of faith I took to put that journey in words allowed me to me re-experience all that again. Hindsight being the teacher it's billed to be; composing this book helped me recognize that for much of my career, I had been uncovering, assembling, and advancing ideas on what it means to be a designer and what it takes to make ideas happen. By conscious act or circumstance. What is required from me, and from those I am (t)asked to work for or with? What's it all for—or rather: what does it all *mean*?

Here's something to know about me: I am a self-proclaimed *'Graphicdesignosaurus.'* I'm a rare breed. An endangered species. I graduated before computers ruled the world. As much a stranger to myself as to the world I ventured into, society found itself in the starting blocks of the digital evolutionary sprint. Designers such as myself, graduating in Graphic Design, had no idea a meteor was on a collision course with the notion of that thing I just learned to do.

---

[1] Have a look at www.graphicmeans.com

Prelude

My career began as a visual artist for a mail-order catalog brand, spray-glueing layouts together. Manual labor. No vectors used, and no one had ever written the word 'trackpad.' A mouse was a biology term. Screens were left untouched in the process of shaping a page of communication. Designers today are amazed by what we once had to do with our hands. My tools[1] were tracing paper, Rotring pens, rolling rulers, Letraset sheets. Strangely shaped utensils to press type-forms onto meticulously measured grids. I had a drafting brush, which played an important role in this primitive production process. It ensured that the rubber eraser crumbs were kept clear of the working surface and prevented crooked lines. I worked at a Mutoh drawing table, which—as a sign for things to come perhaps—was most comfortable to use while standing. My prized possession was a Schaedler ruler set for all typesetting measurements. These were so precious, I kept them in their silver foil-coated cardboard packaging, inside their plastic wrappers. No one was using these but me, they cost a fortune (to me). My most used tools were lead pencils and ruling pens such as an offset swivel pen for smooth curves or the innovative twin-line pens for drawing two parallel lines at once. I loved these as the line thickness as well as the spacing of the lines for each pen head were fully adjustable. The craft I could demonstrate with these twin-liners, along with a drop compass for ruling the small circles parts for headlines I was asked to design, all made me feel a needed specialist. Each are tools of my trade that have since died a gradual and then sudden death.

Fast forward to today, I now work as a principal designer for an Experience Design company. Where we use evidence-based insights and creativity to help people make better decisions for themselves. My industry labels what I do today as UX: User Experience. But for me, the U part is irrelevant. Everything we do, make, think, talk about, or decide upon offers an experience. Be it brand, strat-

Counterintuitivity · making meaningful innovation

egy, space, product, service or, yes, user. Most of my work is in digital and technology, but I also tackle things like Strategy, Service, and Organizational Design.

My work gets made digitally as well. Mouse-clicks instead of eraser crumbs. Virtual zoom instead of medieval looking boxes to project an enlarged version of your drawing. Compared to the first job I had, you could say that I received no formal instructions on how to be that kind of designer. And that nothing taught back then is of any practical use today. I would argue that you're only half right. Obviously, more than a few things changed. Both for myself and for the industry known as Design. Some values remain firmly rooted, however, I believe that we were much more fluent in true collaboration back then. Today, I would label the efforts between design and the clients, as well as those among the design disciplines, as being mostly cooperative. Once we started centralizing the making of design onto the island of a computer, we lost the true art of collaborating.

Desktop publishing, we named it at first in reference, perhaps honor, to the old ways of preparing publications on the top of a drawing desk. We once needed different disciplines to all provide their speciality, honed toward an agreed upon direction or vision, and dove-tailed together by the visual artist—or graphic designer—on a surface of sorts. We do all that now without ever needing to step away from a screen, most of us making our own decisions regarding those different disciplines. Collaboration has changed. Creating has changed.

Change. I reached a point where even that was nothing new. I've seen change before. A few times already—old ways of doing things replaced by better ways of doing the same things. Or, that is what we are to believe; that change is always for the better. But that change can be messy. Being a designer by trade, I've seen this messiness happen in the pursuit of the creative, and the hunt of the innovative. And despite the continued change of doing things, we are still awash in jargons, methodologies and navel gazing. Those in innovation, designers included, never seem to come out of their existential crisis. Clients never seem to embrace the promised value of innovation. The same questions keep coming back. 'What is this job we're doing?' 'How come we're not understood?' The latest change is that companies, governments, if not whole economies, are asking our help to have people adapt a culture of design. What's that *really* about? What gift does the designer give to that world?

I'd like to believe designers should love change. That they comfortably embrace today as a beta for a better tomorrow. It allows us to explore the cutting edge of where design and technology intersect and make ideas happen. We've always done that; objects we call ordinary today, say that supercomputer in your pocket you make calls with, were unimaginable a short while ago. It makes me wonder and gets me excited thinking about what tomorrow's ordinary will be.

The world we live in is changing at a relentless pace. A pace set toward innovation. Sometimes with intent, more often by accident or circumstance. A time of pervasive automation, personalized but ultimately anonymous interactions. An overall Amazon-ization of the online/offline experience. Computers are moving up in the cloud, into our environment and even inside our own bodies. The technologies we innovate, and then design with, or for, are not only changing what we do; they are changing who we are. Everything we design has a human imprint on it, yet I rarely come across peers that understand how that privilege comes with responsibility. And how to safeguard human values and meaning in the act of designing innovations. Someone at Tinder decided you can swipe away the people you want to exclude from your world, anonymously. Bypassing the physicality and accountability of such an act. You're granted permissions to ask Alexa or Siri anything with no need to say "please" or "thank you." How is that going to influence how people will treat those in the service industry?

The algorithms we design curate our social media feeds to make us hide our imperfections and fake our authenticity, so we can perpetuate the prescribed and predictable examples of a like-worthy life we cannot call our own. A life where we hide our mistakes, struggles, and rough edges. What values are we watering down with no conscious afterthought? What if our current efforts in innovation are eroding away our humanity?

Our own human contributions are beginning to appear unreliable, clumsy, and wasteful. Predictability, precision and efficiency are becoming standard measurements of value and success. For businesses, hunger for top-line growth has never been stronger. The belief among executives in the potential of innovation has never been greater. Investment in such innovation programs has never been higher. Amid all that, consultancies declare that creativity and imagination are both desired and required skill sets to differentiate from the automated and artificial.

The cold shower of it all? Innovation's failure rate in most industries has never been higher[2]. We're awash in the mediocre, repeatability of a trend or technology. We pattern abstract pieces of data so the predictable helps algorithms anticipate and react faster than humans would. And then call all that 'meaningful.' If one thing is

---

[2] https://www.publicity.com/marketsmart-newsletters/percentage-new-products-fail/

Prelude

becoming abundantly obvious, it is that ideas and ambition alone aren't warranting an innovation to succeed.

The world we live in and work for will never be slower or simpler than it is today. Industries are changing at lightning speed—new categories, new technologies, new disciplines, new normals. It seems as soon as we embrace them in full, they're old news. So, how does anyone maintain their sense of direction—or better yet, get ahead of this chaos? This is shared chaos, it's part of everyone's professional life. And it is a never-ending journey. For clients, teams, for you. Now that the tech, consumer, and design fields are converging, I believe we need to make a mindset shift and create a future that looks more human by tech, and not less because of it. Our role as innovators is to explore a future that by definition is uncertain, unpredictable. If we continue the path of only thinking about the short term, the repeatable, the measurable, the known and the familiar, then we are no longer asking questions about the future. We will fall short of our potential. It's a big ask. It's easier to accept that nobody can change anything, that society is too big, and an individual is less than nothing. However, it is individuals that create change—together.

This book will question some unquestionable dogmas about design and innovation. I anticipate it will present thoughts that will reflect your point of view, or oppose it. I may have you lose touch with what you hold as an understanding of design and innovation, or what the width and depth of these encompass, in my view, of course. I would not want to have you feel you were less than knowledgeable before reading all this. If there is that sentiment, I propose that this is evidence you successfully shifted your perspectives, and made a step toward more deeply understanding the act of creating something of meaning.

Counterintuitivity · making meaningful innovation

Why do I want to speak to you about this, you wonder? Fair question. For over twenty-five years, my experience as a designer has shown me that the view you adopt—of yourself and for yourself—profoundly affects the way you design. Those I work with or for, are usually in search of meaning. Most designers and innovators I meet want to make a difference. All are looking to become everything they can be and accomplish the things they value. That was my journey. One with highs and lows, with stubborn resilience, setbacks, soul-crunching changes, and paralyzing doubts.

In my career, they told me three times I do not belong, I have nothing valuable to offer, nor do I have the creativity required to make it in this industry. Despite all that, in 2011, CBS Weekly honored me as One of 50 Design Innovation Pioneers in China. Yes, the market that is half a world ahead of everyone else. Schools and academies now regularly invite me to share my message with their faculty and their students. In workshops and conferences, I help people connect the dots to find their own meaningful creativity, and how to activate it collaboratively. Facilitating, if not orchestrating, these acts requires a new generation of creative leaders. People who work with people who never consider themselves creative or innovative. And yet we are all both, disproportionally, yet each in our own meaningful way.

Whenever change happens, there is opportunity. Often it feels like the house of cards we designers or innovators built and called 'reputation,' 'credibility,' or 'meaning' is under constant siege. Perhaps that is a feeling most familiar to you. Maybe the options of what you can do in innovation or design feel limited. I want to propose that you can find a different path, one that doesn't feel scarce or limited. I did, and I believe it is my secret to being in this industry that would have appeared alien to the person I was at the start

Prelude

of the last decade of the 20th century. As a child, I was inspired by Ancient Carthage's legendary general Hannibal, who is believed to have said, "I find a way or I make one." The path I made is one where abundance lives alongside my own innate and intuitive creativity, combined with that of those around me, leading to meaningful innovation. It's a change I seek to create in more of us, it's a gift I seek to give. I cannot mandate how that change will happen for you, but I can stage the conditions in which it could.

True innovation delivers gifts of meaningful change. What gift are you going to give the world?

Part 1
The matters of innovation

"because the ones
who are crazy enough
to think that they
can change the world,
are the ones who do."

—Steve Jobs for Apple's 'Think Different' commercial, 1997

Counterintuitivity · making meaningful innovation

PART 1 • THE MATTERS OF INNOVATION

chapter 1
Human
By Innovation

PAUSE AND LOOK around you. The reality you are perceiving and experiencing has been made. Apart from that which nature provides without any human intervention, everything else is human-made. The creation of things with spaces, textures, and materials are outcomes of inventions and innovations. The actions we do with these, the meanings we gave to and associate from them, the value we bestow in them; these are all acts of design.

For us humans, it is a designed world. It always has been. With the increased visibility of that thing named Innovation, it is easy to think we haven't done much of it prior to the industrial or modern age. That notion is not something I subscribe to. What we in our history often define as discoveries are instead innovations that are the outcomes of design acts. Obviously, early man did not make distinctions nor job titles to identify the designers among themselves. Instead, our human tendency was to be adept at observing nature and then appropriating from it. Appropriation was our first act of design through which we invented and innovated.

01 Human by innovation

One of the most significant appropriations from nature is fire. We did not 'discover' fire; that was in plain sight and occurrence, and our planet experienced fire long before humans were on it. Evidence of fire in the fossil record, referring to the long geological stretch of time before humans, is based mainly on the occurrence of charcoal. The oldest fire recorded on Earth has been identified from charcoal in rocks formed during the late Silurian period, and that has been set at around 420 million years ago. Though plants had already spread on the land surface at that point, the fluctuating levels of oxygen in Earth's atmosphere meant that the first major wildfires recorded occurred later, dating from around 345 million years ago. But it was the spread of grasses and grasslands such as the savannas of Africa, around seven million years ago, that made the biggest impact. Not only on the environment, but also on the animals living there. Savannahs need regular fire, or else the vegetation may convert to scrub and forest. In this context, and with the knowledge that the African savannahs were home to early humans, it is believed that they would often have seen fire on the landscape, and the first 'discovery' would have involved seeing and following the fire.

Our ancestors' first interaction with fire probably came following a lightning storm that started wildfires. These would cause animals to scatter, likely making them easy pickings for early humans waiting on the edges of the affected areas. Other animals, such as hawks, are also known to engage in such behaviour. There would have been several natural behaviors to observe that gave early humans moments of appropriation. Also, once the fire had subsided, the burned landscape would have allowed for easier foraging. Charred, dead animals left in its wake may have been collected. Some of the foraged food would have been "cooked" by the wildfire, making it more edible and nutritious than when raw. Powerful, hungry brains need calories, and cooked food provides more calories than raw food. Fire helped intelligent humans evolve. That evolved intelligence then went about conditioning the use of fire. Because wildfires occurred only sporadically, the next step would be to learn how to preserve it. Here's where humans started to exhibit the innate ability to extend their appropriation talents into conscious, measured, and deliberate thoughts for which they had a repeatable plan. They imagined and then designed solutions.

Fires were first sustained by assigned *'fire preservers'* who used slow-burning animal dung. Those in charge of protecting fire were believed to be solely dedicated to that act. A first primitive division of laborers if you wish; this to can be labeled an act of design, or even an innovative decision to ensure an improved outcome. A fire would have been useful not only for light and warmth at night, but to frighten off predatory animals, and the smoke would have been effective in keeping insects away. All conducive to human well-being. This ability to 'stretch' fire through invention and innovation was a novel skill, only developed by humans. So much we can reasonably speculate.

Eventually, early humans solved the issues on how to create and manage fire. Given archaeological evidence, this likely occurred no earlier than 700,000 years ago and no later than 120,000 years ago. With all that in mind, there is factual evidence that managing and creating fire was done differently and multiple times over by early humans in various locations all over the world. This again debunks the notion that it was but a discovery, and that it had more to do with an increased ability for humans to plan and execute a series of predetermined, repeatable actions to arrive at a predictable result. In this case, make fire. Anyone who has ever attempted making fire from sticks and dried grasses will appreciate the effort that this requires. The design of fire by humans as a convoluted process took place over a long period of time. Using and controlling fire on a regular and widespread basis may have started only 7,000 years ago. This may have included the use of fire for land clearance for agriculture and even for warfare. Before we habitually made and used fire, before we had the conditions for us to control it, several acts of innovation through design were required.

Humans displayed their capability, first, mostly through appropriating what they observed in nature, and then by a pure natural ability to design things they imagined without the inspiration their surroundings would give them. Forked branches were used as utensils, stones were fashioned into clubs and knives, the fur of an animal as augmented skin for our own. However, no wheels exist in nature. Unlike branches, stones, or the animal pelts, there was no appropriation that could hint to the possibility of a wheel. The wheel is a one-hundred-percent-human innovation. We did not stumble upon it; we *designed* it.

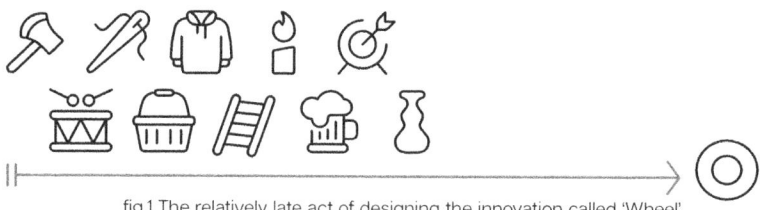

fig.1 The relatively late act of designing the innovation called 'Wheel'

Designing the wheel was a relatively late act of innovation (fig.1), in fact, several other significant human innovations predate the wheel by thousands of years: bow and arrow, sewing needles, woven cloth, rope, jewelry, calendars, maps, glue, basket weaving, boats, beer, and musical instruments. It took humans a lot more time to design the wheel. The innovation of the wheel for transportation is the classic example of early human ingenuity. A quintessential

Counterintuitivity · making meaningful innovation

innovation that distinguishes Homo Sapiens from all other animals and kickstarted civilization. But in the scope of human history, the wheel is a rather young innovation. The first recognizable wheels were actually not even designed for transportation. Evidence shows someone created them to serve as a potter's wheel around 3500 B.C. in Mesopotamia.

This period we know as the Bronze Age, which is a relatively late chapter in the story of the development of human civilization. By this time, humans had already innovated and designed the planting of crops, how to herd domesticated animals, and had some form of designed social hierarchy. The use of wheels for pottery making may date even further back into the Neolithic. As mundane as it appears, the ability to create and shape a pot, a vessel, was of meaningful significance for humankind. It was only possible once we figured out the innovations needed to manage fire. Making things from burned clay has been part of the human experience for thousands of years. A small figurine of a woman is the earliest known object made of fired earth, dated to almost 30,000 years ago. The earliest known example of a pottery vessel was made around 18,000 years ago. Since then, the craft of pottery has developed in all parts of the world, both for the practical purposes of making usable vessels for food and storage and as expressions for art and rituals. About 7,000 years ago, the Egyptians designed their innovation for glazing pots, enhancing both appearance and functionality. The Chinese steadily iterated their kilns to produce more and more highly decorated stoneware and porcelain. The immense strides in making pots were the result of design thinking and innovations by thousands of potters over thousands of years.

And one such innovation was the potter's wheel. There are many ways of forming a pot. Hand building is the earliest method and is still widely used. The potter's wheel is said to have been designed about 7,000 years ago, and it is still in use today as the most practical tool in consistently shaping vessels out of wet clay. It would take another several hundred years before humans figured out how to use a wheel for transportation. You could say it took awhile to get things rolling—pardon the pun.

Spinning wheels are basically useless unless they're attached to a secure structure of some sort. It was only after mankind finally built such stabilizers—which we now call 'axles'—that the wheel began realizing its full vehicular potential. The wheel-and-axle concept was the true meaningful innovation. That idea required extreme finesse, which only metal tools could adequately provide. Such craft and skill were not widespread until somewhere between 5,650 and 5,385 years ago, hence the delay. The Bronocice pot, a piece of pottery discovered in Poland and dating to at least 3370 B.C., is believed to feature the earliest depiction of a wheeled vehicle. The evidence suggests that small wagons or carts, likely drawn by cattle, were in use in Central Europe by this time in human history. One reason that mankind did not just discover the wheel, but innovated it, is that wheeled vehicles appeared in various areas across the Middle East and Eastern Europe. The invention of the wheelbarrow—a one-wheeled cart used to transport goods and raw materials—is usually credited to the ancient Greeks. However, earlier evidence of wheeled carts has been found in other parts of Europe and in China. Unlike the lightbulb, there is no one person to claim the wheel as their invention. Making it more appropriate to label it as an innovation.

Wheels, of course, are still used today to facilitate all kinds of shipping and transportation. While the basic function of the wheel is unchanged, modern wheels are much different from the simple wooden wheels of the past. Innovations in materials science have made possible all kinds of tires for bicycles, cars, motorcycles, and trucks—including tires designed for rough terrain, ice, and snow. While the wheel is associated primarily with transportation, it has other applications. Watermills, for example, use wheels—large structures with a series of blades along the rim—to generate hydropower. In the past, watermills powered textile mills, sawmills, and gristmills. Today, similar structures called turbines are used to generate wind and hydroelectric power. The spinning wheel is another example of how the wheel can be used. This device, innovated in India over 2,500 years ago, was used to spin thread from natural fibres such as cotton, flax, and wool. The spinning wheel was eventually replaced by the spinning jenny and the spinning frame, more sophisticated devices that also incorporate wheels. Gyroscopes are navigational instruments that consist of a spinning wheel and a pair of gimbals. Modern versions of this tool are used in compasses and accelerometers. Wheels even became design metaphors in language; think "being the fifth wheel," or "the wheels are coming off." When Shakespeare wrote King Lear, one of his characters proclaims, "Fortune, good night, smile once more; turn thy wheel!" The wheel is such a marquee human innovation that we even define it as a final solution. There is, after all, no need to reinvent it, but true to our human nature, this hasn't stopped us from attempting to do so.

Modern human beings are the result of millions of years of evolution. Not just physical evolution: we are also the result of a series of innovations and inventions of technology that make our lives liveable today. These human innovations began 1.7 million years ago. Pointy pieces of stone or bone fixed to the end of a long stick were used by humans to hunt animals or fight with one another. Archaeologists found projectile points made of bone dating to ~60,000 years ago in the Sibudu Cave, South Africa. This was sophisticated tool crafting. Before we could craft such projectile points, humans

01 Human by innovation

had to invent, and then innovate, a whole range of stone butchering tools. The Acheulean hand axe is arguably the first tool we hominids made, a triangular, leaf-shaped rock, probably used for butchering animals. The oldest one yet discovered is from the Kokiselei complex of sites in Kenya, about 1.7 million years old. The concept of such hand axes remained virtually unchanged until ~450,000 years ago. Clothing, bags, sandals, fishing nets, baskets: the origins of all of these and lots of other useful things require the invention of textiles, the deliberate processing of organic fibres into containers or cloth. That was a very different approach from skinning animals and using the fur as blankets or clothing. Albeit textiles are difficult to find archaeologically, for obvious reasons, there is circumstantial evidence: net impressions in a ceramic pot, net sinkers from a fishing village, loom weights and spindle whorls from a weaver's workshop. The earliest evidence for twisted, cut, and dyed fibers are those from the Georgian site of Dzudzuana cave, between 36,000 and 30,000 years ago. Notice how the act of textile weaving brings together a series of inventions and innovations; devices, tools, dyes, and a known, repeatable process that is teachable. It is the halo effect of invention and innovation; new proposals and possibilities, new ideas and new meaning.

The appropriation of fire by humans was not done by discovery, nor was the wheel a one-off invention. By defining properties of intelligence and craft, which separate us from other animals, humans applied their innate ability to design their own humanity. We innovated our human-ness. Each innovation had a person forming an idea of what could be a great addition to the world people lived at that time, and then they gave it existence. A new shape or form, an added function, and more significantly, a new meaning. One such person is a 16th-century Welsh mathematician, named Robert Recorde, who invented the common equals sign when he had tired

Counterintuitivity · making meaningful innovation

of writing the words 'is equal to' and sought a less onerous way of conveying the meaning. Choosing a pair of parallel lines of equal length was an inspired solution and a brilliant example of [graphic] design's power to solve a practical problem. There are countless other examples of adroitly designed symbols. And not all are designed from scratch. The digital incarnations of the hashtag and @ symbol are equally successful examples of design appropriation, rather than an invention. But all are beautiful acts of design, sometimes resulting in new inventions, other times experienced as meaningful innovations. It always astonishes me that so many people still fail to appreciate those qualities. I find design endlessly fascinating because it is richly contextualized and constantly changing, forcing me to continually reassess my understanding of it.

Invention or innovation; what then is the distinction between them? In its purest sense, **invention** can be defined as the creation of a product or introduction of a process for the very first time. It was thought and formed by someone, or a group of people who collaboratively figured something out. It's unknown and unproven and done because of the possibilities of that time. Innovation, on the other hand, occurs when we improve on or make a significant contribution to an existing product, process, or service. This significant contribution or repositioning of an invention falls under that. I won't go much deeper on this example, as countless books and articles do it better justice, but what made the iPod, and the music ecosystem it engendered, innovative wasn't that it was the first portable music device. Nor was it the first MP3 player. Apple wasn't the first company to make thousands of songs immediately available to millions of users. What made Apple innovative was that it combined all of these elements—design, ergonomics, and ease of use—in a single device, and then tied it directly into a platform that effortlessly kept that device updated with music. Apple invented nothing. Its innovation was creating an easy-to-use ecosystem that unified music discovery, delivery, and device. And, in the process, they revolutionized the music industry. Innovation requires invention. Consider the microprocessor. Someone invented the microprocessor. But by itself, the microprocessor was nothing more than another piece on the circuit board. It's what was done with that piece—the hundreds of thousands of products, processes, and services that evolved from the invention of the microprocessor—that required innovation.

Innovation: that other I-word. The term is so willingly thrown about, so broadly interpreted, it lost a bit of its luster. Asked what it is today, you likely hear that innovation is the process of translating an idea or novelty into a good or service that creates value or for which customers will pay. In business, innovation often results when ideas are applied by the company in order to further satisfy the needs and expectations of the customers. Innovation comes from the Latin *innovationem*, noun of action from *innovare*. The Etymology Dictionary further explains innovare as dating back to 1540 and stemming from the Latin *innovatus* "to renew or change." Innovation can therefore be seen as the process that renews something that exists and not, as is commonly assumed, the introduction of something new. Furthermore, this makes clear that innovation is not an economic term by origin, but dates back to the Middle Ages at least and possibly even earlier. The central meaning of innovation really relates to renewal. For this renewal to take place it is necessary for people to change the way they make decisions, they must choose to do things differently, make choices outside of their norm.

It might be the mantra of business today, but the irony behind the king of buzzwords is that, originally, 'innovation' wasn't a compliment. It was an accusation. When the term *"novation"* first appeared in thirteenth century law texts as a term for renewing contracts, it wasn't a term for creation—it referred to newness. In the particularly entrenched religious atmosphere of sixteenth and seventeenth century Europe, innovation was grounds for excommunicating a person or denouncing a doctrine. In 1636, an English Puritan and former royal official, Henry Burton, began publishing pamphlets advocating against church officials as innovators. It didn't work out for him. It was the church that accused him of being the true "innovator" and sentenced him to life in prison, but not without first cutting off his ears.

Innovation began taking root as a term associated with science and industry in the nineteenth century. The term paired up nicely with the forward momentum of the Industrial Revolution. However, the innovation of that period focused more strongly on invention, particularly technical invention. In this time period, it was the term invention that enjoyed status as a buzzword. Several factors helped invention earn its prestigious and positive meaning. There was now a rise of the first consumer culture, increased numbers of patents to take ownership of the invention, and strong government focus on building labs for research and development toward 'discovery and invention.' The differentiation between invention and innovation can be attributed to Austrian economist Joseph Schumpeter[3]. In 1939, he defined invention as an 'act of intellectual creativity undertaken without any thought given to its possible economic import,' while innovation happens 'when firms figure out how to craft inventions into constructive changes in their business model.' In other words, inventions were intellectual properties, innovations made these profitable.

Recently, a new element was woven into this understanding of innovation making something novel into a commercial proposition;

---
[3] Joseph Alois Schumpter's Creative destruction
https://en.wikipedia.org/wiki/Creative_destruction

the bringing to market a new technology. This was especially tied to government funding for research and development in laboratories and foundations. From the early 1950s until the 1980s, innovation was understood as a process: theoretical research in labs provided an initial foundation; applications of that research were devised and developed; and from there, they became commercialized products. Innovation was thought of as a packaged, predictable research product, and government funding for these kinds of ventures directly corresponded to the rise of this understanding of innovation. For roughly 100 years, from about 1870 to 1970, the economies of the world brimmed with newness.

Since then, with the exception of the worldwide adoption of the internet, the forward march of technological progress has hit something of a dry spell, regardless of all the talk about innovation. What has been achieved, however, is a greater ability to manipulate information which has an outsized effect on the lives and work of a relatively small segment of the population. These people happen to be the folks that spend the most time talking about innovation, though: designers and entrepreneurs. But has all that talk led to better, more forward-looking innovation? It seems to me that we need to improve the way we talk about innovation. We're going to do it anyways, so we should try to do it right. Look at the period from 1870 to 1920, or maybe 1940, and think about how unbelievably creative and powerful that output was. Although actual innovation might be in decline, mentions of innovation are resurgent. In an interesting twist of history, the word also seems to have transformed into shorthand for "anything new and/or good." Google's useful Ngram database of word use finds that not only is "innovation" suddenly a bigger deal than "invention," but also total mentions have reached an all-time high. Meaningful innovation might be on the decline, but for some reason, we just can't stop talking about it.

Counterintuitivity · making meaningful innovation

Inventing and then designing innovations is one of humanity's oldest activities. Better still; it is a natural human ability. That ability has determined our humanness, we have designed ourselves to become the most dominant species of the planet. Each of us is designing most of the time. Reading these lines, at this moment, you are busy designing thoughts and narratives based on the words on this page. You are assigning meaning to them. Both my writing and your reading about design are acts of design. This book is an act of design by itself. It won't be a surprise for you that I hold true to the notion that everyone has the ability to design and innovate, albeit in varying degrees of capability. Because there are among us a group of people for whom this capability is practiced, honed, and crafted— also by design. For whom the act of innovating is at the forefront of not only what they see, think, feel, and do, but why they see-think-feel-do. For whom design is a very conscious, engrained, and visceral activity. A calling, some would say. A character trait, others. And when you do this activity mindfully and with full awareness, it gradually and then suddenly becomes a way of being. Those with an entrepreneurial tension, the ants-in-the-pants jitter to make or imagine something. Preferably something new, or at the very least, something meaningfully better.

Designers. Innovators. Perhaps you consider yourself one of them (in which case; *howdy*, fellow traveler!). However, it is not a prerequisite to imagine something meaningful. We all have that ability. Inventions are made by imagination, innovations are made by design. Design is a human ability that allows us to define and shape the world the way we choose to experience it. As such, we have designed our world to be '*our*' world.

01 Human by innovation

Counterintuitivity · making meaningful innovation

PART 1 • THE MATTERS OF INNOVATION

chapter 2
The Thinking and Making of Signs

OVER THE YEARS, I've often noticed that the concept of design is surrounded by quite a lot of confusion and misunderstanding. And it is not only ambiguous by those outside the realm of design; I have found this confusion to live among designers and innovators as well. What does 'design' mean? I'm well aware that many have tried before to explain and define design, so this is not meant to be 'just another explanation.' Instead, it's a way of presenting design that I have found useful to explain its value and what I believe are its key principles.

To begin, what comes to mind when you think of design? For many of us, the word conjures up thoughts of creativity, products, architecture, graphics, the aesthetics of something. These are all valid responses and encapsulate what are known as traditional forms of design. Forms that sit close to the origin of the word '*design*'; the thinking and making of signs. In the 1350s, written English records started to use the word '*designen*,' derived from the Latin word '*designare*.' What can be understood as to "mark out, devise, choose,

02 The thinking and making of signs

designate, appoint." Composed from '*de*'- "out to" and '*signare*,' "to mark." Signare comes from '*signum*,' Latin for "a mark, sign." *Designen* in these English texts was a verb, meaning "to designate." To determine, to mark out or plan: a form of thinking in other words. Later, the 1580s, French texts began to use the word '*desseign*,' of which meaning was closer to the end-state of the design process; the word was a noun. Put together, design is about both the cognitive and the tactile; the thinking and making.

But today, the practice of design extends beyond these to encompass broader techniques, and when we talk about design in the field of innovation the focus is more cognitive with terms like '*strategic design*' or '*design thinking*.' To me, design means developing distinction. Working on sustainable, effective, and meaningful solutions. Back in the middle ages, there was no difference between a '*maker*' and a '*designer*'; the two activities were combined in one person. Think Leonardo Da Vinci. It was the industrial revolution that separated the two. In today's innovation landscape, the trend is toward combining the two, with the option to be a 'maker' increasingly more important.

Yet, those who think about things are positioned higher within society, while those who make things are relegated to the lower tiers of society. White-collar/blue-collar, in other words. This continues to play out today; the polarity between thinkers and doers. This polarity extends in how we work with and use ideas and creativity. By extension, it determines how we innovate and improve the products we deliver, downstream, all the way to the societies we innovate for, upstream. We judge ideas and creativity against polarizing variables, such as intellect versus emotion, relevance versus rigor, concrete versus abstract, proven versus possible. This separation, and these polarities, are fundamentally influencing the way in which we un-

Counterintuitivity · making meaningful innovation

derstand, see, determine and justify any act, role, and outcome of design—and how we innovate.

I assert that the skill part of this equation, the physical making of a design, is the rightful domain of those trained and schooled in the execution and production of design plans. These designers are not a commodity. Turning ideas into products with personality requires a mix of imagination, artistry, and efficiency that takes years to become second nature. Add to all that using these skills while also testing, negotiating, adjusting, and with that, solving implementation problems. Even the *'making'* of a design has its demands, and its conditions are not immune to changes. The making part of a design is now deemed at risk for automation; robots doing the job. Just as the arrival of the Macintosh computer—way back. It was to converge and democratize design practices. For all practising designers at the time, computerization necessitated an extensive rethink of the craft: no more mechanical artwork, no more paste-up, no more typesetters, no more expensive retouchers. Many of the tasks previously done by reproduction houses were taken over by designers sitting in front of computer screens. It was the beginning of a new age of digital self-reliance and a period of massive reorientation. Just as with the arrival of the internet. Here was another new way of thinking about and making a design.

Suddenly, designers no longer had complete control over how their work was received. The inability to control browser use, screen ratios, and fonts had a decisive impact and old rules such as the number of characters per line-length rule became redundant. Even the users themselves could mess with the appearance in ways unthinkable to designers trained in print design where layouts were fixed once they left the designer's hand. These two events each threatened to shrink the role of the designer, yet the opposite happened.

02 The thinking and making of signs

There are now more graphic designers and students than ever before. Design is a global industry embedded in, and inseparable from, business and culture. For many, graphic design is as much a lifestyle choice as a career choice. People do it because they love it.

Despite history showing design and designers can be said to have benefited from these two pivotal moments in history, there are concerns that the craft and the profession might not survive quite so well now that AI is in the mix. Is the surge toward a fully automated world about to engulf design? AI-driven design already has the potential to remove some, or most of the production-based tasks that designers do. Need a thousand web banners for a global ad campaign, all with different information and numerous languages? No problem. Robots capable of handling such routine tasks will result in fewer design production people. It might seem that automating the innovation or design process is impossible. In reality, the process is already underway; in China, Alibaba offers Luban[4], an AI-powered creative content services, proposing hundreds of layout variation in minutes. Clients pick, choose and obtain their campaign material in less than half an hour.

Anything that can be automated, will. Soon, the production of design now in the safe pair of hands of trained, skilled craft-minded professionals we call designers, will no longer be a fact. Eventually, and just as human beings have learned to do since the introduction of industrialization, craft-only designers must adapt. Only those with learning agility and a growth mindset will find longevity in the making of design; software titles come and go. By the time you have gained proficiency in one, there is a new-same-but-better program to learn. It's my belief that designers-at-heart are well equipped to adjust and adapt. If a designer is truly who you are, it doesn't matter

---

[4] https://www.alibabacloud.com/blog-alibaba-luban-ai
-based-graphic-design-tool_594294

how the industry shifts, your design soul will carry you through. It is very important to deal with digital technologies, which have their place and their importance but certain impressions, the beauty, and uniqueness of things can never be realized without a craftsman who is able to dialogue with a material. Product development is preceded by prototype manufacturing. In other words, artisan production is always part of industrial product development—the work at the computer is of primary importance, but craftsmanship and manual work will always remain. That said, flexibility and a willingness to learn may be the biggest challenge facing the world's craft-first designers.

The variety of design domain holds disciplines we still call '*traditional design*': architecture, interior, industrial, engineering, graphic, information, fashion, interaction, software, product, etc. There are '*non-traditional design*' fields: systems, organizational, service, social, educational or even healthcare design activities. But each of these acts is the integration of thoughts and actions through design. And that integration should cause the ability to imagine 'what is not yet real' and then do 'what is needed to manifest it into a reality.' If it solves a known problem, then what is not yet real has the potential to become a welcomed innovation. If it explores what is possible, it can lead to a difference-making invention. At all times, the common ground for each attempt is to provide something of meaning. As the eternal optimist, my challenge to creatives is to adapt. Machines are skilled at recognizing patterns, but humans are skilled at disrupting them. Investment in AI will only increase. But what you can do as your creative, human self is find the intent within all of these experiences and bring meaning to the forefront. Design in a way that brings the human back in.

One way to do this is to adopt a human-centred approach to design. The thinking and making of a human-centred design during

02 The thinking and making of signs

the act of innovation is about exploring the known conditions in order to to offer a solution to a known problem. Whereas invention explores the possibilities of the imagination and is likely to be more a solution that is still looking for a problem. Invention is often the work of a single inspired individual, most often rooted in science, and limited to the research and development department of the organization. That said, there are innovations by individual acts of design, by those who posses a craft or material understanding; someone who has identified what he or she feels is a problem that can be made better, or could enjoy an alternative to its current solution. It's a problem opportunity they first see and then make their act of design a self-inspired, self-motivated innovation—and not always a human-centered one. They then introduce their innovation the world as a suggestion, declaration, or sometimes even as an act of rebellion.

Some of these are proposals we could define as a redesign; the redoing of an object in an attempt to correct and renew our experience with that object. Take, for example, the work of Shigeru Ban[5], known for designing buildings using paper tubes. In our minds paper is fragile and flimsy. A commodity material which we hardly spent time contemplating. Ban has found enough strength and durability in this material to design permanent, inexpensive buildings. At the Expo 2000 in Hannover, he built the Japanese pavilion using paper tubes, creating a grand arched space, while allowing the entire structure to be recycled after the event. Though inventive in its application, what Ban offers is a new way of thinking and looking at a material such as paper. He does that kind of thinking and looking to re-imagine the concept of an object. One such re-imagined concept is Ban's proposal of a redesigned toilet paper roll. His alternative to the universally known object was to have a square paper tube form

---

[5] http://www.shigerubanarchitects.com/works.html

the core of the roll. Because the core is a square, the roll has a natural resistance, functioning to reduce the over-use of the resource. It would also prevent any momentum from spooling the traditional round roll, which happens with a light pull. In addition, packaging square rolls saves space in transport and storage. A single redesign, a solution seen by the mind of a practitioner of innovation, resulted in a design outcome that offered meaningful change. These are interventions on ordinary objects that are so overly familiar, we could no longer see them. A questioning, critical mind does still see them. These are people who offer a different understanding of how we relate with the subject or material matter they reintroduce. Their proposals offer something meaningful to those willing to engage with it.

Making such proposals and exploring new possibilities do not always require products or services. Art helps my design practice by providing a broader source of exploration or even knowledge. Not everyone agrees that knowledge can be found in works of art, modern or not. The problem is that when we think of knowledge, we often only think of 'scientific knowledge.' The proven, the commonly accepted 'truth.' Artists working today may find themselves in an uneasy position, unsure of where art fits in a modern scientific, tech-enabled world. For me, especially those artists working with a strong focus on current, emerging and future technologies, such as Joshua Davis[6], Sougwen Chung[7], Michael Manning[8], and Petra Cortright[9]; at their core, each is ultimately striving to uncover and highlight qualities that seem innately human—such as empathy, intuition, and unspoken forms of communication like gesture, touch, rhythm, and motion. Their works consider what distinguishes hu-

---

[6] https://joshuadavis.com
[7] https://sougwen.com
[8] http://www.themanningcompany.com
[9] https://www.petracortright.com/

02 The thinking and making of signs

man nature from the tools we create, while also serving to underscore that even these tools are inherently a part of us, as they are also a product of our own imaginations.

I firmly believe in the individual's right to identify their work as they wish, whether as design, art, craft, anthropology, or whatever. That said, I find the old-fashioned assumption that design is somehow inferior to art to be deeply damaging. If, like me, you believe in design as a powerful and productive medium that can help to build a better life, it stands to reason that we need the best possible designers to do so. We are not likely to get them if design is seen as so marginal a discipline that its practitioners are eager to distance themselves from artists. Also, the richer, more diverse, and inclusive design becomes, the more compelling it will seem, thereby enabling it to attract the high caliber of designers that society needs. This makes design one of the most powerful forces in our lives. Ultimately, I echo what graphic designer Paul Rand said about art as a consequence, not an intention. Design is intent made real.

Design innovates. And because innovation aims to introduce something with intent, design is the vehicle through which it operates. Today's condition states that it originates within society. The essence is in the process of discovering a problem shared by many, and then manifesting a solution or alternative for it. And because the problem is within society, many more people need to be included in understanding plans for solutions as well as the processes for solving the problem. What that yields are new variables, new roles, and new conversations. Because while the designer is important to the act of innovation, he is not the sole owner of that act of design. At its heart, design is about the betterment of our lives: aesthetically, experientially, sensorially, or emotionally. For some, the criterion is simpler usage, others look for what makes things more comfortable, more beautiful, or more exciting. This purpose to improve on a known condition is what makes design go hand-in-glove with the act of innovation.

But do we understand enough about the act to design innovations? To understand something deeper does not require us to define it better, or describe it more accurately. We can take something we think we already know and shift our perspective so that the unknown part of it comes to light, appearing new and fresh, and inviting a deeper look. That is what this book is attempting: for us to shift perspectives on what we held firm as a certainty, so that a new possibility, a new future, can be made possible.

Why? Today designing something innovative is based on a multitude of complex criteria: human experience, social behaviors, global, economic, and political issues, physical and mental boundaries, and a rigorous understanding of people and their cultures. Manifesting innovation into existence requires yet another collection of criteria: capital investment, market share, production ease, growth, distribution, maintenance, service, performance, quality, ecological issues, and sustainability. There are a lot of moving parts; different expertise, priorities, systems, and structures. How these are navigated and addressed will shape any act of innovation.

The considerations needed of all these factors shape—read limit—are acts of innovation. It is those acts that give us objects, inform our forms, our physical space, visual culture, and our contemporary human experience. These quantitative constructs shape business, brand, society and the value they hold. To be valuable, innovations must have a meaning. Meaning is, after all, a collective human need, we all desire it. Even those who are creating and designing innovations are seeking the meaning of that act. The thinking and doing of what signifies a betterment is a compelling and all encompassing drive.

With all our human capabilities and potential to be aware of our own thoughts and actions in relationship to everything else, planet included, we should be living in an entirely different world—one that is full of inspiring objects, spaces, interactions, and experiences. But that hasn't truly happened.

PART 1 • THE MATTERS OF INNOVATION

chapter 3
Unsuited For Uncertainty

OUR WORLD IS not yet holding an abundance of truly inspiring objects, spaces, and experiences because, increasingly, the way we think and act in the pursuit of innovation has resulted in processes that look the same, and result in the same; a limited return on user-centric ideas. The two pillars of innovation, as introduced by scholars, practitioners, and business leaders, state that to be innovative, you need to generate as many ideas as you can as rapidly as possible. And that you work *outside-in*; with understanding users and the problems they wish to have solved.

These processes are still heralded as the ideal methodology but are proving less ideal when working with uncertainties. It's largely because we apply old thinking to new and unknown matters. It's outdated to think we live and work for an economy of products and services. The world demands experiences and outcomes. In this era of social and mobile technology, customers, employees, suppliers, and partners are in direct communication with one another. Those personal networks and the brands they're passionate about influ-

03 Unsuited for uncertainty

ence their decision making and their spending. Our workforce has changed, too. Employees expect to be able to determine when and how they work, the technology they'll use, and the values their company declare. Innovators can take part in this conversation only if they recognize how and where it's happening. And it's not happening as much as we think it does when engaging in the process of innovation

It's time to talk more about Design-Thinking, that kid heralded as 'new on the block.' It promises to be the key between doing something with a purpose; an innovation with meaning. Design-Thinking is, however, fundamentally conservative and preserves the status quo, that very thing innovators wish to change. More often than intended, it is reactionary and thinly defined on 'insights' that prove to be but observations only. The enthusiasm around Design-Thinking, and its adoption by firms and consultancies influence how we innovate today.

And that momentum is now slowing, as shortcomings are surfacing, and a fair degree of reservations on the potential of this 'tool' is bubbling up. Skepticism about Design-Thinking is now seeping out onto the pages of business magazines and publications. That Design-Thinking is poorly defined; that if it is thinking, then it is not a tool; that the case for its use relies more on narration than data; that it is little more than basic common sense, repackaged for a hefty consulting fee. The process tends to favor participation and input from those who know the most and marginalizes those who know the least. As some of these Design-Thinking concepts have found their way into the world of policy, and social change efforts have been rebranded as social innovation, the discomfort around this approach has now begun to surface in the field of public policy and even education. I see all these friction points as valid.

However, I observe most who call out the technique for its shortcomings miss the main default with Design-Thinking. It is, at its very roots, an old established strategy to preserve and defend the status-quo. When firms task the job of Design-Thinking to the consultancies and designers, it immediately privileges these practitioners above the people they are asked to work with or for. Limiting their participation in the design process. In doing so, this pivotal tool limits the scope for truly innovative ideas, and makes it harder to solve challenges that have a high degree of uncertainty or complexity. This often scales the innovation effort back to doing things the way they have always been done; a sure recipe for disappointment and negating the entire effort that saw the need for this kind of thinking.

To understand why Design-Thinking is unsuited for uncertainty, it's important to look at its origins. Where today we are to see it as a method that is as innovative as the solutions it promises to produce, Design-Thinking strongly resembles an earlier model of problem-solving, celebrated in the 1970s and 1980s for the superior solutions it was supposed to produce. Far less marketable, the technique was named "Rational-experimental Problem Solving." [10] It, too, was enthusiastically embraced by companies and designers, and was the spark to reshape practices and methodologies in firms and across government. Design-Thinking today is a watered-down version of this problem-solving methodology. Similarities between both methods are such that Design-Thinking can be seen as a bit of a knock-off. Rational-experimental Problem Solving was built around a series of stages, each leading up to the identification of a needed solution. Likewise, Design-Thinking is generally described as phases that cover the ideal design steps. Nothing out of the ordinary unless you take a closer look at the actual phases.

[10] https://www.rasch.org/rmt/rmt74h.htm

03 Unsuited for uncertainty

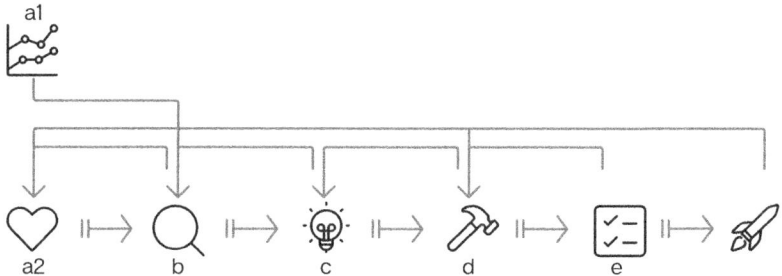

fig.2 comparing Rational-experimental Problem Solving and Design Thinking

Rational-experimental Problem Solving began with the notion that finding a solution starts by canvassing existing "data" (fig.2 a1) about the problem. Design-Thinking proposes that the designer should generate information about the problem, by drawing on their experience of the people who will be affected by the design through the empathetic connection that is established with them (fig.2 a2). This phase is one that design thinkers tend to favor: "empathize." Therein, another issue comes to light: empathy for those who are affected by the problem-to-solve is established as but a phase. A time-bound period in the process to innovating the solutions for them. This slight divergence of using existing data, versus generating it is the only practical difference between these two approaches.

The next step in both approaches is where the working team is to "define" the problem or design challenge (fig.2 b). Next, both approaches suggest moving toward developing a theory about how to solve said problem or design challenge (fig.2 c). In rational-experimental Problem Solving, this step is labeled the "hypothesis" phase, while Design-Thinking calls this phase "ideate." Then, both methods will advise trying out the preferred solution (fig.2 d). It's "implementation" in the older approach, but most of us today will know it as "prototype." The final step in both methods is to evaluate the effectiveness of the proposed solution (fig.2 e). For both the "evaluation" phase of the rational-experimental model and the "test" mode of Design-Thinking, the iterative aspect of these approaches to problem solving is set in motion. Both methods suggest now using the data gained from this phase to return to earlier phases of the process in order to refine either their hypotheses and their solutions, or both.

This may have burst a few bubbles for those unaware, but 21st century Design-Thinking is the same-but-different as 1970s-80s Rational-experimental Problem Solving. We're doing our problem solving in essentially the same way as before the use of computers, internet and digitalization. Does Design-Thinking still sound like the true way to go about innovating?

Recall how those who think about things are positioned higher within society. That was prevalent in the 1970s as you would expect it to be. With Design-Thinking mirroring the methodology established by thinkers, both approaches implicitly establish problem-solving as the activity of the powerful; the thinkers. Both techniques turn the everyday ability to solve a problem into a rarified practice, limited only to those who self-consciously follow a specialized methodology, and therefore perform at a premium due to that specialization they hold. When problem-solving is a capability that every human shares with every other human. Granted, there are those trained and practiced at the complicated or complex, yet specialized techniques regarding thinking usually serve to shape solutions by agenda and resource constraints. In such cases, the 'winning' solution will not necessarily be the better one. Depending on the variables in the room, only the solutions that are favored by the powerful, or at a minimum by the influential, get to move forward. Both rational-experimentation Problem Solving and Design-Think-

03 Unsuited for uncertainty

ing provide fertile grounds for this political risk to pollute innovation itself.

Looping back to that one difference between Design-Thinking and Rational-experimental Problem Solving; the former celebrates ambiguity as a precursor to any solution. By not starting with existing data, in some ways, that's a good thing. Ambiguity can be a construct through which true curiosity is generated, and can set the stage for all possible questions and ideas to be considered. But for this to happen, an aware Design-Thinking practitioner needs to helm the effort. Without this, Design-Thinking reinforces the privileged position of the designer for whom ambiguity should be more familiar to work through. Designers are seen as the instrument that cleans messy ambiguity into the sleek lines of an elegant solution. The bridge over which all the implicit understandings that make it into the final design must first pass. Moreover, because they themselves generate the understanding used by connecting with potential users during the "empathize" phase, whatever needs of product users and communities were perceived are refracted through the designer's personal experience and priorities. His or her background of obviousness. Bias—as any ethnographer will confirm; subjectivity is inevitable. It's a human tendency to see things through our own lens and experiences, even when the effort is to try to see it through someone else's.

That is why disciplines that rely on empathetic engagement for data collection must stress the importance of paying attention to the practitioner's identity and political positioning. The Design-Thinking method does not, however, underscore this need. This omission signals that the designer, as a creative visionary, is somehow suspended above the fray of bias, blind spots, and political pressure.

As a result, step one of the process to find innovative solutions is blurred by how the problem is seen by those privileged to see it.

The trouble with privileging the role of the designer, or even a small circle of innovators, is that their imposed bias—conscious or not—inevitably narrows the potential for innovation. The true value of ambiguity is found in the spectrum of meanings that friction up against each other when a problem is still undefined, and from the opportunities for new connections those collisions evoke. Design-thinkers should celebrate these connections, especially those that span very different perspectives, disciplines, and categories of things, and view this kind of abductive reasoning as core to creativity. When the designer acts as a gatekeeper for the meanings that are included in the design process, the potential for these connections becomes limited. Not only to what the designer views as significant but also to the relationships he or she can imagine. Innovation will not be seen or found beyond what the designer can observe or identify.

Design-Thinking has allowed us to celebrate conventional solutions as breakthrough innovations but—in most cases—sees us all continue with business as usual. The late Alan Stacell[11], a prolific artist and former professor emeritus of architecture at Texas A&M, said "People are only capable of two things: Building boxes and tools to make more boxes." It can be a parallel statement about innovation and its ever-increasing library of methodologies in order to deliver said-innovation. Practitioners, designer or consultants alike, have never been short of processes to promise our clients that we can squeeze the potential out of any idea, brand, service or product. Housing that promise is a term we made up in our collective imagination: Design-Thinking. It made innovating visible, catchy,

[11] https://digitalartarchive.siggraph.org/person/alan-stacell/

03 Unsuited for uncertainty

and marketable, and it has certainly delivered and contributed to the success of recent initiatives. At the same time, however, it has fast-tracked itself into a sort of one-size-fits-all process, a closed space only the privileged can contribute to because it is they who determine the quality of the thinking.

A focus on output quality also challenges a key tenet of Design-Thinking—that managers can think like designers. On one level they can. Let's agree that all of humanity are designers, and that design is one of the things that separates us from the apes. First, when we talk of designers, we usually mean professional designers who have reached an accepted level of competence. They have survived a Darwinian selection process (there are far more graduates than jobs) and have clocked up well over 10,000 hours of practice on projects. Contradictory to the Design-Thinking mantra, designers learn by doing, not by practicing a theory. Designing innovation involves a lot more tacit knowledge than in other areas of business. It's therefore hard to believe that senior managers can change their thinking habits of a lifetime after a workshop or two working with designers. And, to be frank, to suggest as much devalues what designers do.

We are unable to fully predict, despite each new scientific discovery or technological invention, the complexity of the systems that are at play and the shifts on the horizons for them. Yet it is for those challenges that Design-Thinking is advertised to deal with, offering formulaic and rigid solutions. However, if leaders in this process have the gates to this design space flung open to include meanings that users and communities view as significant, we would surely read fewer stories of design interventions gone wrong. These variables and properties of Design-Thinking are problematic enough on their own, but the repeatability of this method is increasingly proving itself to be particularly ill-suited to solve problems in

Counterintuitivity · making meaningful innovation

rapidly changing areas, or those with lots of uncertainty. Said differently, Design-Thinking as a process makes it unsuited for solving uncertainties. In Design-Thinking, once a design has completed its "ideate" phase, the space that allows for ambiguity and new alternatives is shut down. Which is a shortcoming to the intent of the practice whether we're talking about its origin as rational-experimental problem solving or not. It often meanders into frustration and detachment, with both consultant and practitioners taking shortcuts back to the assumptions they wished to avoid in the first place. But not all can be blamed on faulty methodology. As the 1982 Fun Boy Three song goes, "'Tain't What You Do (It's the Way That Ya Do It)." Not all problems are design problems. While the methodology is expanding the range of what design can help solve, not all problems an organization wants or needs to solve are suited for design to solve them.

Where design can help is to better understand the problem, reframe it, or waterproof the thinking that can help direct to a solution. Designers love questions, but what they should really love is to reframe the questions. It is then soon understood that this way of thinking is not a process, it is a culture. The majority of companies are still archaic in their organization, whose people perform under imposed ceilings. The thinking required for innovation requests that any and all contribute and take ownership of ideas and solutions. The harsh reality is that for most companies, the practice is really nothing more than entertainment; the team bonding workshop, that nice break from corporate meetings and delegation management.

It is not helpful when Design-Thinking gets billed as a one-size-fits-all tool by those who advocate the use of it. When thinking about innovation, it requires looking beyond a to-do list. It's an all-in sort of deal; everything upstream and downstream have to be open to being considered. Yet most corporations, teams, and even the consultants hired to negate these issues, all struggle to actively avoid their tunnel vision, and look beyong assumptions. Design-Thinking is rooted in rational, while creativity is emerging out of intuition. Rationalilty and Intuitivity are polarities that both have a part to play in the process of innovation. However, the comfort, efficiency and profitability is more visible when rational is leading the conversations and ideations. In addition; it shifts the majority of attention to those experiencing the issues, versus those tasked to solve them. That is at odds with an employee's day-to-day KPI (Key Performace Indicator)chase.

Lastly, the term 'thinking' is wrongfully understood as to avoid any doing. However, the faster the design doing starts, the better the design thinking becomes, the stronger the potential to truly innovate a solution. By prototyping as fast as possible, and iterate from there, problems and solutions are better defined and understood. Done is indeed better than perfect. Trouble is that both designers and innovators are alike here; both want the glory of the brilliant idea. To avoid only addressing symptoms, and instead find new meaning and possibilities, the entire system of product-service-brand-operations has to be investigated and open for change. It's not the solution, it's the problem that innovators and designers need to fall in love with more. But it's hard to stick with problems long term. It requires a shift of focus. That we move from the idea that designers simply create usable components and product designs, to the understanding that their work impacts the perception of entire brand and customer experiences by making meaningful proposals.

Every company, every team, has their own understanding of what design is and what the role of designers should be. Within the innovation field, there are so many specializations within design

Counterintuitivity · making meaningful innovation

roles—engineer, strategist, interaction designer, information architect, motion designer, prototyper—and these roles can have overlaps with other domains such as marketing, architecture, industrial design, or even sound design. At the industry level, the understanding of design and what designers do has evolved. For companies, innovators, and consultants, the recommendation to embrace a messy, inclusive process of interpretative engagement, to say nothing of championing open solutions that sustain and encourage participatory creativity with their design, may seem unworkable or profligate.

But, as true practitioners of design or innovation, we need to hone our abilities to match the changes that we cannot yet imagine or fully comprehend. That starts by daring to make innovation meaningful again. It also starts by rethinking the role of those who practice design and innovation.

03 Unsuited for uncertainty

Counterintuitivity · making meaningful innovation

PART 1 • THE MATTERS OF INNOVATION

chapter 4
Now That Earth Is No Longer Flat

WITH THE CALL for more ideas for innovation, design is having a red carpet moment. Tech, consulting, and financial firms are snapping up design agencies left, right, and center. I am currently employed with an experience design agency that recently became part of a large tech firm. You now see designers moving into CEO roles, or holding C-suite titles such as Chief Design Officer. A study[12] by the Design Management Institute, or DMI, delivers evidence that, over the last ten years, design-led companies outperformed the S&P 500 by a whopping 219%. It's no wonder design has become more important to business than ever before. It's a vehicle by which brands can express themselves across an increasingly complex ecosystem of spaces. Design-Thinking is billed to solve complex business challenges. And it's the means by which brands build emotional connections and immerse customers in an effortless world that they have helped orchestrate for them. The thirst for innovation has given design practitioners a seat at the big table.

---
[12] https://www.dmi.org/page/designdrivesvalue

04 Now that the earth is no longer flat

It is now a common occurrence that design has a leading role in the pursuit of the innovative. It is as if the corporate world came to the realization that, contrary to their old beliefs, the world is, in fact, not flat but round. That there is no edge at the end of the ocean. For a few brands, it still feels a little awkward and suspicious, but for a majority, there is a rise of conviction—and volume—in their voices that design is an integral part of their world, and that they are transforming their world to no longer be flat, but round. All enabled by digital and design.

If that sounds unflattering or belittling of me to call non-design-minded people out like that, let me clarify that, from where I am sitting, designers and innovators are not much more advanced in the view of their own world.

Think about your studio, workspace, or office environment. What is in it? You'd be right to shortcut to 'people and stuff.' Desk, chair, computer. Air, light, humidity. Scents, sounds, surfaces. And, people, yes. Those Jim Morrison poetically captured in their essence: "People are strange." We very much are. A lot of the things we talk about, and a lot of the things we assign meaning to and value, exist only in our own imagination. It is a very normal phenomenon. It's human to have and use a variety of things that do not actually exist except in our imaginations.

Take, for example, money. Specifically bills. It's but paper and ink that we recognize as money. But the concept of money only exists in our collective imagination. And that collective mind has agreed that this paper and ink has a value. We've collectively accepted that without much question. It's a globally scaled act of a grounded assessment, that some of us even see as an assertion—a truth. Because if I give you a bill of ten Euro or US Dollars, you can

Counterintuitivity · making meaningful innovation

go to other places and use the collectively understood value of that piece of inked paper. And everywhere else, it will be worth ten Euro or ten US Dollars. However, there is no such thing as money, in a real-world context. Money does not exist in a biological or chemical construct. It's not real, it's only paper and ink, that enjoys a mutually agreed upon assumption. That it has monetary value.

Paper money was introduced by the Tang Dynasty in China in 740 B.C. They made paper money as an innovation of the invention of block printing. Block printing is much like stamping. Used as the process for quilts, the government made ready use of it in printing money. They made paper money because when coins were devalued, they became too heavy to carry. My point is that money is a designed concept only. We made this up.

Agile, Scrum, Design Thinking, Backlogs, Sprint, Lean, Story Points, UX, Personas, Strategy, Flows, Journeys, Stand Ups, Research, Hypothesis, Synthesis, Brain Storming, Ideating, Workshopping, Facilitation, Divergence, Convergence... If we look at all these design terminologies; all are made up by us-designers. None of this exists outside our imagination. As with money, these things have a collectively assumed value and meaning. Without that collective assessment, none of these things actually mean anything. The fact is that these design things we talk about actually do not exist. And yet we are strangely fixated and protective of these terms. We expect—if not demand—clients and outsiders to willingly accept that these are valuable, meaningful things. Precious to us, but really only because we imagined them to be so; claiming these to be of benefit to companies and their customers. I want you to free your mind of these trivialities. I want you to let go of the importance you think these have. It's time more people, especially those in design and innovation, shift perspective.

04 Now that the earth is no longer flat

Open up any text editing software, or any program where you can use differently designed fonts. You'll recognize an R, right? How do you know that? Well, as a matter of fact, you've seen a whole bunch of Rs, and you've now generalized and abstracted all of these and found a pattern. Once you see a pattern, you cannot unsee it, and you know an R when you see one. It may not be your everyday R, but you will understand that it is one. What I'm saying here is understanding and changing your perspective are linked together. That's my claim here; you only understand something if you have the ability to view it from different perspectives. When I give someone else another story, a metaphor, an analogy, if I tell a story from a different point of view, I enable understanding. If you are a designer or innovator, and especially if you are a UX practitioner, this thing about changing perspectives should sound more than familiar to you, because you do it every day. It's called empathy. When I view the world from your perspective, I have empathy with you. If I really, truly understand what the world looks like from your perspective, I am empathetic. And that is how we obtain understanding.

Because it's important to point out that our perspective of something, and our understanding of it, are both deeply interlinked. Only a few hundred years ago, and after we collectively accepted the evidence that the world was not flat, it became commonly accepted and understood that the earth was the very center of the universe, and that all known heavenly bodies—including the sun—rotated around it. Old celestial maps visualized that belief and illustrated how, with the earth at the center, the known planets circle around it. If I think about people living at that time in history, holding this view of their world, I'd say their perspective would have restrained and limited them from what they could have been able to learn or discover. It was clear, however, that back then, people would have been firm in their beliefs that this was the truth, and no other possibility can or even needs to exist.

We've since evolved our perspective and understanding of our actual place in the universe. That we are orbiting around the sun which is but a star in a solar system. That system moves around among others in an interstellar system, forming the milky way galaxy, itself a part of a larger galactic cluster of many other galaxies, the collective of which make a supercluster, and these combine with countless other superclusters resulting in what we can observe as, and name, the universe. Most of us today hold a radically different perspective than our ancestors six generations ago. That new perspective totally changed what we think is possible. So then, I ask: What does the design universe truly look like? Where are we today in truly understanding it?

It's September, and we're approaching the midway point of a six-week engagement to help define a digital transformation vision for a large utility company. Their industry is changing fast, not only with the decarbonization of electricity production, but also with the rise of new startup brands that offer virtual electricity grids. The company employs top tier talent in renewables and data science, and have made strides in repositioning themselves, but the bigger challenge is to create a new digital-first culture, become innovation-led, and have all that be of inspiration to both employees as to investors and analysts. Their ambition is that their corporate website is the first expression of the new vision. So far, so same—these are comfortable waters for myself and most of my team. We've helped plenty of brands in various different categories find their voice and purpose in 'becoming digital' as to optimize the conditions for innovation and bolster defenses against disruption.

04 Now that the earth is no longer flat

Preparing for a workshop meeting with the client team, established professionals in their respective fields, yet most were new to the terms 'experience design' and 'digital transformation.' The overall effort was strengthened with the brand appointing a Chief Technology Officer, who hired a UX (User Experience) specialist for in-house representation of the discipline, and the methodologies involved. Wanting to visually represent a framework for the diverse project team to understand how we-consultants were going to handle the challenge and guide them along, I Google-image-searched 'UX model.'

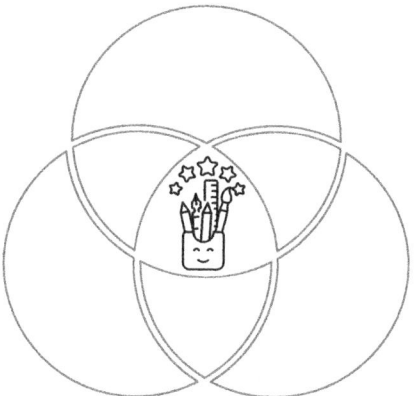

fig.3 the fallacy of the design-in-the-middle Venn-diagram

The search built a thumbnail mosaic. Largely tiled with visuals of the same Venn-diagram (fig.3). Three circles intersecting. The top one for 'technology,' under it 'business' circles, either left or right, and then 'users' would neighbour that. And in every single diagram, in the middle overlapping segment, there was the label 'Design.' Scrolling the page, dozens of differently colored, yet similarly composed, Venn-diagrams reaffirm the same formula. Three systems to intersect, with the shared middle design. The axis around which everything else orbits. Design self-appoints dead-center of everything. I've drawn my share of these myself, have instructed others to do

Counterintuitivity · making meaningful innovation

the same, and made variations of what the outer circles are, but design is always in the middle. And everything known orbits around it. Like those old celestial maps, made by people who we portray today as blissfully ignorant.

It's a world view that only lives in our imagination. Does design truly require or deserve the condition to be the center of everything else? If we think about design this way then, just as it did for our ancestors, it sets your perspective, influencing all your consequent behaviors, attitudes, and actions. And all we see and look for is the pattern of belief that we have come to accept. The models we use for design, the frameworks we establish as to innovate are all the same. Design in the middle, with business, technology, and users at the outer perimeter. All pivoting around the design thing. If we think this way, it sets our viewpoint and determines all our behaviors and consequent actions. Just as we've come to understand it, centuries ago, the reality of the world is that design is not in the center of everything.

The systems that designers center themselves in all have functions that bring important values and meaningful contributions to the bigger picture—the universe—of a business and all its related problems and opportunity spaces. But as designers and innovators, what we do is spend all our energy in that one small sphere of the vast expanse of the real world. All our questions, all our conversations and efforts, are all focused on this one little particle, this granular speck on a sandy beach. Practitioners talk about design and innovation, write about it, explain it, mostly to and among ourselves. It's self-sabotage; we're only acting on our own behalf, interests, or agenda. We're mostly seeing things from our own existential crisis, needing the comfort of being seen as the pivotal axle around which the corporate, technological, and human behaviors are in motion, for us-innovators to inundate a project with endless ideas and propositions to solve problems. It's an antiquated belief system for a world that has revealed itself much different.

The arenas that interact within the spaciousness of innovation are known: Sales, IT, Marketing, Analytics, Customer Support, Engineering, Project Management, Human Resources, Research, Developments, Finance ... all these functions and disciplines are valuable to the success of a business and the success of their innovation efforts. All are all equally important, but are all seen as equally important? All these functions have leaders and sponsors, and all these people form groups that talk, meet, decide. And ultimately what they decide has been informed by how they view their world. Companies who have their leadership made from one of these business departments will likely not see the other areas, including design, with the same importance and value as they see theirs. Brands with a leadership formed from sales will be prevalent to matters of acquisition and retention. Finance-groomed leaders with profit and loss. Do we-designers recognize how this influences and halos throughout an organization, when we are preoccupied with establishing ourselves as the center mass?

All these roles and functions matter fundamentally, and design is not the center of this. **Leadership is.** The initiative, direction, and attitude of leadership is the true guidance around which all other units orbit. Leadership provides gravity for each of these units that consists of their own micro universes; Marketing breaks up into Events, Public Relations, Product, Brand, Strategy, Research, etc. All with their leaders and world view perspectives.

If you're like me, you now realize that the majority of your career may have been spent talking to yourself. Asking the questions

Counterintuitivity · making meaningful innovation

to and acting upon the answers formed by yourself. Deciding the values and meanings associated with the ideas you yourself came up with, for the problem you wanted to solve or improve upon yourself. And by yourself, I mean among and with the other beings in your universe: designers and innovators. Even among those with whom you share your world view, there is often tension. It's researchers versus strategists, visualizers versus technologists. That tension, on what discipline matters more, offers more, creates more; that rigidity is the lens through which we see the world. It's the fingerprint of innovation today.

If you adopt the new view of your world, it brings a different field-of-depth, and a different understanding of what your role in it needs to be if you aim to make things more meaningful. It requires you to take a leadership role. Even if that requires you to go beyond your assumed or appointed role. Approaching the work as a leader allows you to create the possibilities to talk to all others involved. To gauge their perspectives, hear their questions, and with it gain an understanding of their thinking. Leaders open up conversations that, once heard and felt, bring about true inclusiveness and integration.

Taking a leadership role. The mere mention of it has a majority of designers, especially those with limited experience, conceal themselves in the scavenged mollusk shell they carry around like hermit crabs. And I get that. Leading is a loaded term in business. It auto-equates to hierarchy. A construct we-humans designed, to arrange items (objects, names, values, categories, etc.) with the intent to distinguish those items as being "above," "below," or "at the same level as" one another. Hierarchy is an important concept in a wide variety of fields, such as philosophy, mathematics, computer science, organizational theory, systems theory, and the social sciences (especially political philosophy). Regardless of the established or perceived hierarchy in play, bringing meaning to the act of innovation requires taking up the role of leader.

Old English *lædere* "one who leads," agent noun from lædan, is a title for the head of an authoritarian state, formed by hierarchy. However, I want to position Leader or Leading with the meaning "writing or statement meant to begin a discussion or debate." **Taking the initiative to form a hypothesis,** for the main purpose to discuss and converse about it. Not to solve or define, not to determine or dictate; but to facilitate understanding, alignment, and inspiration.

One of the most powerful acts of a leader in design or innovation is to routinely reset what I call the "background of obviousness." As we each think and act from within our own world view, our obviousness is composed of deep-seated belief systems embedded from past experiences and our culture, language, and education. Much of this obviousness comes from the grounded assessments we hold within that world—our collective imagination of things that we take as known truths. However, there's no such thing as obviousness. This isn't, of course, itself obvious; nor is it clear why it should be a problem. Acting similarly to how background programs run in the system software of a computer, if unchecked or invisible, our obviousness loops endlessly, blurring and bending our thoughts, emotions, and awareness. It is how we pour the reinforced concrete in the foundations for our own cognitive biases. The operative question is how do you investigate and overwrite these deeply rooted belief systems?

At the risk of sounding—well—obvious, the most immediate step you can take is by not taking anything as being passively understood. By becoming actively aware, most often these patterns and blockages that are hidden from our view can be visible to others. By questioning, contemplating, or validating the assumptions. That in itself can be experienced as uncomfortable by those making such an inquiry. Even by those who have a naturally higher sense of awareness to what others hold as obvious knowledge. I am currently working alongside a very intuitive, highly aware colleague, who serves as a senior consultant on our projects. She has shared with me how vulnerable she could feel asking about or exposing what is sensed as obvious, such as dails about industry-specific circumstances that could make her come across as ignorant or inexperienced. It's going through this initial resistance that any practitioner can establish influence. My colleague has done this enough times to find her own voice when allowing a re-envisioning of perspectives by those in the conversation. What is satisfying to watch is that the experts caught in their obviousness are usually accommodating and forthcoming with their point of view and then recognize the need for a re-alignment with the belief or value that obstructed a deeper understanding.

But first, establish your own blinders to the obvious. Here are simple awareness practices for your own experimentation; signs you, as a designer or innovator, are thinking out of your obviousness only. Thinking that Marketing will use what it is you design or build. That you present this solution to them, that they will understand it, and that—double-click of the heels—innovation happens. There won't—nay cannot—be any questions, doubts, or refusal because you did your part. Or, thinking a Finance department is only involved to make sure the bill is paid. Not that people working there had more involving priorities such as safeguarding the health of the company and honoring their commitment to the financial well-being of the staff. Thinking people in Sales have the worst practices, care the least about their customers, and are only driven by num-

04 Now that the earth is no longer flat

bers and bonuses. Whatever we provided as solutions will undoubtedly do their job for them. Maybe you are seeing Customer Support as the most boring of jobs, completely replaceable by the solutions you can design for them, and all in desperate need for you to have their service models redone. Or, that those HR folks just have to deal with the shitty, messy ego problems. The ones you hope you are never asked to solve.

Thinking this way is—in all seriousness—naive, biased, ignorant, and prejudiced. I was fortunate, but only in hindsight, to have learned this lesson very early in my career. But first, I was too busy to realize the learning because I was too busy explaining to others what I do, what they should do, or what I should be allowed to do. Many designers are hard-wired to control their environment, so much so that design is often steeped in a yearning for power. It's an occupational hazard of sorts, and for the majority of us it is never intended to be malignant. Take an information design project, like a road signage system or a subway map, which is intended to be entirely beneficial by helping others make sense of our surroundings and guiding them safely and efficiently from place to place, ensuring they arrive at their chosen destination on time and unharmed. We are controlled by the design of the signage or map throughout that process, in a benevolent way.

In 1994, I joined a company called MacLine[13]. Based in Brussels, Belgium, it was a precursor to what these days is called a 'start-up.' The two founders started this venture during the last year of their university studies, as part of their thesis. They sold Apple Macintosh hardware, and a portfolio of software titles and other accessories, to Belgium's graphics industry. The desktop revolution had yet to reach

---

[13] MacLine Belgium was acquired by Easy-M in 2012 and now operates as Switch

fever pitch, and three years in, the company was expanding. They wanted bilingual support for their sales. Their interest in me was that I had a bit of prior experience in working as a visual artist for a mail-order brand. You see, MacLine operated as a mail-order only vendor. There was no storefront, instead, they occasionally sent out a black-and-white printed catalog to a subscription base. Our desks were in the warehouse, in between the boxes and shelves of the merchandise. Clients called or faxed their orders and questions in, and we consulted pre and post sales. The support group, our technicians, sat in the same space, feverishly upgrading RAM capacity or figuring out why the SCSI connection of a zip drive was faltering. It was unglamorous and looked unprofessional. The warehouse would get overwhelmingly hot in the summer and cold enough during winters that you worked with a fleece hat on. There was barely any money for marketing—which worked to my hiring attraction. I had—in their words—more hands-on experience producing a successful mail-order catalogue, I was myself a graphic artist and therefore their target audience, and I already knew enough about hardware and software to make a convincing sale. In one breath I was named Sales, Marketing, and Customer Support manager all in one.

My days consisted of taking calls, either by request or by luck of picking up, offering guidance to prospect or existing clients, doing the admin of a sale or post-sale support, including repairs. During the slower parts of the day, I worked with the founders, both only two/three years older than myself, to compose the next catalog. Now with me aboard, they could more frequently commit to publishing, and soon we had a monthly schedule. We went from an eight-pager to 16, then 32. By the end of my second year, we produced one quarterly 64-page and two 32-page booklets, before upgrading to a full-color version for the 32-page format. We had doubled the headcount, expanded into the Benelux, became an au-

04 Now that the earth is no longer flat

thorized and preferred Apple vendor, and had plans for markets in Germany, France, and Spain in the works.

Laurent and Gregory's, the founders, ambitions were not limited to MacLine. In 1995, they invested in another 'startup'. Our warehouse was upgraded and, resonant with the sound of, modems; they were investing in Belgium's first internet provider, Skynet[14]. In 1998, Belgium's national phone company, Belgacom, acquired Skynet—keeping the name for the program. Skynet and MacLine were seen as linked; we were among the first to consult and guide Belgium's businesses and governments on all things internet. In 1996, MacLine's ecommerce site went live that year, and, through experimentation, we had figured out how to connect FileMaker Pro (our sales software) with site. We could offer live updates on availability and status of an order, delivery, or repair. It was 1996. In '98 we moved to a three-story building, annexed to a warehouse space that was thrice the size of our original one. We housed, within our team, Belgium's first e-commerce corporation that facilitates consumer-to-consumer and business-to-consumer sales through its website, as well as a gift-giving e-commerce group[15]. Both got acquired by eBay. Other initiatives we made was creating the email platform mail.be, which got acquired by ContactOffice

My job had evolved to mostly the marketing and communication needs of all three of these companies while staying the contact person for a select group of clients. My experiments and blunders with what was known as 'multimedia,' together with the constant interactions I had with clients, prospects, suppliers, vendors, colleagues, shaped how I saw the role and meaning of the act of design. And that it was my mistake to have the belief that design should be at the center of everything a company does. Prior to joining this

---
[14] Skynet is now called Proximus Skynet
[15] Opendeal and Gift.be

company, I believed that as a designer working on behalf of that company, I should be at its center. That made sense to me for at that time. Working in this unique way, the bigger picture unravelled. Sales talks to customers every single day. Designers or innovators do not. You could argue that this is different. Sales teams talk to people to sell, and we designers talk to people to learn. I can tell you from first-hand experience that sales teams talk to customers for that very same reason: to learn. As a top performer in a sales team for a company, I had to learn to talk to learn. Already in 1995, through Sales, I had insights, data, reports and learnings on what worked and what didn't.

More and more businesses are now focusing on relationships with their customers. This may have you nodding your head as confirmation that, for a business, that makes perfect sense. Then why not for a designer who works with and for these businesses? Brands that sell products without the intent to be reachable, transparent, and supportive are not going to be doing well if they are going to do anything at all. Those who push, annoy, or fail to deliver a meaningful experience, simply won't survive. How many of us in design or innovation talk to Sales to learn? Is that department even represented in the innovation team? Any member of a sales team will know the customer and the product better than the product or innovation team. The same applies for any support team. They know your product's failings better than you do. Meanwhile, designers talk about design, about its importance, and about the need to be pivotal. We spend an awfully long time mapping and advocating the user journey, or plotting the customer journey. When in reality, every human, including those we work with and for, is on a journey we know very little about.

04 Now that the earth is no longer flat

What we don't do enough is talk to understand. We hold firm to the belief that we, designers, are the voice of the user. It's a lie we tell ourselves; we are *but a voice* that could offer a representation of that user. Because it is a voice that lives inside of ourselves. That voice is our thoughts brought to sound through the lens we applied to see and feel in ways we imagined that user to see and feel. We are an important voice, but just one. One of many voices that make for a true user voice. Just as we ourselves are only one component of many other equally important components that make up a company's innovation act. If anyone, be it designer or innovator, operates under the notion that they, and they alone, give voice to the user, then they are not living in the real world. And the understanding of their version of the real world, along with their role in it, is limited, naïve, and, honestly, rather self-serving. I will repeat myself because it is important: the biggest lie we tell ourselves is that we, and we alone, are the voice of the user. We are not.

Because, in truth, we are rather disconnected from that user. Whenever we apply empathy voicing what the user thinks or feels, we do this out of our own choice of what we want to be voicing out. We speak out of our understanding of how we want the user to see the world. If we keep seeing that world as centered around us, then our biases will determine our own behavior, and the empathy we seek to evidence is only our own. We will only seek what our knowledge can recognize or defend. We will look for patterns or predictability; where we collect, manipulate, and use information to forecast a needed outcome to increase consumerism. I cannot shake this feeling that we have been doing all of this innovation of late, wrong. It brings me to one simple, but hard-to-answer question ... *Why?*

Counterintuitivity · making meaningful innovation

PART 1 • THE MATTERS OF INNOVATION

chapter 5
The Trees And The Forest

INNOVATION IS NOT an abstract or new concept, but the tangible result of the human urge for knowledge and progress. Our drive to question the status quo and to be constantly on the look-out for new ideas has barely changed over the millennia. Above all, innovation simply expresses the human desire for a comfortable life in prosperity, peace, and good health. The longings and ideas of how we can make our lives easier and more substantial accompany us in our everyday thinking and acting. As individuals, we seek meaning and purpose. A reason to get out of bed in the morning, a belief tomorrow is a better day.

The origins of innovation lie in the big and small things of everyday life. These are things that we want to improve or adapt to our changing needs and wishes. The finiteness of resources forces us to develop new solutions. Our human imagination propels us to strive for radically new technologies. We derive questions on how to do this or that differently and find the necessary knowledge. In doing so, we inevitably encounter problems and are confronted with the

05 The trees and the forest

limits of what is currently possible. And that is the genuine starting point for the emergence of innovation: the desire for change and progress by overcoming obstacles and shifting boundaries. We've never been as advanced as we are today, but when I look around, I cannot help but see a world that is more unbalanced, unmatched, uninspired, or unhappier. Surely with our design and innovation capabilities, we can avoid that feeling of spinning out? Designed innovations have been the cultural shapers of our human world from the start. Through thinking and making, we have designed objects, tools, systems, cities, and commodities. But today we increasingly want to innovate systems that alter, transform, recontextualize, and self-interpret their own environments. It's no longer only about images, shapes, form, and words; innovation now influences our social and cultural interactions across societies.

This new condition exposes the boundaries of what works through old thinking and methods geared to preserve the status quo. New choices need to be made. Humans originally evolved in a world of few choices. Prehistoric, preindustrial, and pre-digital eras required far fewer decisions than today's all-access, always-on world of too much information. That age of information has innovation struggle with its central paradox: we must do something each time that appears to be happening for the first time.

And so, by demand and by reaction, we flood our innovation process with ideas, prioritizing the user-generated or crowdsourced ones. Somehow quantity will provide quality. We stumble on ideas by looking outside, by what we call, 'emerging ourselves in the problem space.' Those we talk with, under the moniker of learning, are to provide us with these ideas with which we think solve their problems. People like experts in the domain, users of the device, providers of the service, management of the brand; stakeholders. For all its

Counterintuitivity · making meaningful innovation

banner-waving of being human-centered, ironically, we water down the human-ness by categorizing people under anonymous cards, such as 'stakeholder,' 'persona,' 'user.' Every person has a very individual set of knowledge, characteristics, and wishes. Everyone has skills and valuable experience that can be helpful in a wide range of situations in life—personally and professionally. Thus, every human being has the potential to become a catalyst for innovation and to participate in its implementation. Meanwhile, we seek to empower only the select few to carry on that torch.

The radius of our worldview, our depth of field if you wish, is not any wider or richer than those we work with or for. Yet, undeservingly, most designers or innovators see themselves as the vital missing part of the puzzle. The center point of anything and everything that wants to be of value and meaning. Without realizing it, those of us in such advisory roles often bring our own issues to our work helping others. We make assumptions and judgments based on our own experiences that often have little to do with the leader we're trying to be, or team we are trying to support. I'm worried that the discussion about innovation is losing its vitality and that a handful of beliefs are becoming dangerous dogmas. Two that worry me the most are: Innovation should be user-centered—i.e., users are the first and foremost source of insights. Innovation processes should, therefore, start from observation of mainstream or extreme users. It's lovely in theory, but it is more meaningful to focus on what makes us human, and less on what makes us users. Innovation should be something more than a focused pursuit of creating simpler products—and then wanting this to spark emotional connections with users. Those looking for a prescribed way to implement Design-Thinking are destined to be disappointed. Innovation is a messy, opaque process that depends as much on group dynamics as intellect or insight.

05 The trees and the forest

Our second mistake is that we see the innovation process as more important than the outcome. There is no one "true" path to innovation. Yet all too often, organizations and the designers they partner with act as if there is. They lock themselves into one type of strategy and say, "This is how we innovate." It works for a while, but eventually, it catches up with them as they spiral down the narrow path of iteration. Locked into a set of solutions that no longer fits the problems they need to solve. It's a narrative of becoming square-pegged in a round-hole world. Innovation always loses relevance this way.

Just as it will lose impact when all the responsibility is placed on the design effort. Yes, good design is often made by great designers, but these are talents that are few and far between. The 0.1% of those practicing the profession are the ones who are believed to have the magic silver bullets. User-centered innovation is very effective for incremental innovation but fails when it comes to breakthroughs. Designing something innovative to truly fix a human condition, support or protect them, or understanding them to such a degree that it becomes part of their identity; you'd be forgiven to think there is a supernatural requirement about it all. Let's forget about innovation as a magic process and focus on how designers and managers should best work together to deliver great quality outputs. Just as the marketing department wouldn't rely on a single marketing tactic, or a CFO on a single source of financing for the entire life of an organization, there is a need to build up a portfolio of innovation strategies designed for specific tasks.

It's self-evident, but frustrating, that this is not truly understood: one size does not fit all in innovation. Different innovation problems require different approaches. There is no one method that is always good. The more disruptive or platemaking an innovation is, the more emergent its process. If all companies converge on the same approach, innovation becomes less of a differentiator. The most innovative companies are those that question the existing innovation paradigms that explore new avenues. Today most innovation efforts are really primary efforts in tech-first iterative cycles. Without realizing it, most innovators, designers included, are having functionality tunnel vision. Pushing frantically for the next version of things they have seen before. Innovators and designers help their technologies find a problem rather than problems finding a solution. A more holistic approach to design-made innovation is inevitably becoming the option to explore. Innovating the known is an important half, but opening it up to more is the everything. Design should always be in the service of a better life, but, unfortunately, it does not always achieve that objective. We can all think of examples of design projects, even the best-intentioned ones, which threaten to make our lives worse rather than better. I have yet to meet a designer who wants his or her work to be dysfunctional, dispiriting, demeaning, or disempowering, but sometimes the reality is that it is. Some design projects prove to be damaging because of the way in which they are applied. The computer virus was an innovation, originally designed as a self-replicating form of software that could be installed remotely without the user's knowledge, but it was not intended to be malignant. Quite the contrary. Sadly though, it proved to be open to abuse and to create destructive viruses.

This exposes a blind spot because no one seemed to have considered that self-replicating software can be anything other than useful. And if the alternative downside ever was considered, it certainly was not acted upon. There is another blind spot in plain view today, one that has us questioning what innovation is actually for. In Part 2, I expand on what it is we should call innovation, based on the blind spots surrounding the digital app economies that are currently billed to be improving our lives.

05 The trees and the forest

What I can signal here already is that there is a new path to meaningful innovation to consider, one that better fits our changing world. We're already supplied with a surplus of ideas, yet feel desperately lacking in meaning. It's time to innovate the way we innovate. The old ways do not apply because these are geared toward solving known problems only. This is a point that previous champions of user-centricity now also make. For example, Don Norman[16], a pioneer in human-centered design, recently raised issues about the limits of user-centered innovation, arguing that it cannot create breakthroughs. The developers of the Nintendo Wii[17] didn't get close to users, they got close to 'interpreters': media people, artists, designers, sociologists, retailers, suppliers, etc. Innovating for the future is first about finding the right interpreters of that future.

Innovation might be the buzzword word du jour, but it is hardly a new concept. In fact, it is as old as the human race. A Google search on what it means yields 487,000,000 results in point two seconds. Lately, the word itself has become so prevalent that it's difficult to recognize meaningful innovation from simply an updated idea. Through design and innovation we create what we see, what we use, and what we experience. In this time of crisis and revolt against social and economic imperatives, designers and innovators can choose what they dedicate their profession to. Iterating and ideating on products or services that only aim to increase consumption at the expense of personal data will have us look for what we can predict only.

We need visionary innovation work where we shape new meaning for something that shifts perspectives and environments. Innovation that restores the humanity back into the societies we design for. Things like economic, environmental, or social crises shouldn't

---
[16] https://jnd.org and https://en.wikipedia.org/wiki/Don_Norman
[17] https://artstechnica.com/gadgets/2006/10/wii-2/

Counterintuitivity · making meaningful innovation

really be happening, or be left unmet. Certainly not with the capabilities in tech that we have today. This is the step change required. One that requires a different approach altogether. That requires vision. Designers stuck on a path of incremental change have become less visionary. Spending all their effort in getting close to consumers to find the right answer to a tech problem and then attempting to become businessmen as to try to solve the problem commercially. Those designers have lost vision.

Ouch...

To the best of my recollection, it wasn't until 2010 that anyone ever called me "innovative." But now, I hear it all the time. Often I notice a particular temperature around this statement. That is, I either sense the temperature in the room go up, or down, whenever I am declared to be "innovative" or an "innovator."

So what happened? For a designer, the ability to innovate and quickly solve problems within their project work is one of the strongest values they can bring to the proverbial tables. Companies are looking to hire creative and innovative specialists in the hopes of not becoming stale or falling behind more flexible and agile startups. To stay ahead of the competition, the senior managers within a brand are paired with innovation specialists or advisors, experts who have previously used creative thinking to launch successful projects. However, in labeling enterprising individuals as "innovators," these managers may doom them from succeeding before they even start.

As the person who is looked upon to dazzle with your new creative solutions, all eyes are on every move you make. Every word you speak is heard as a directive, a solution, even a guarantee. But

05 The trees and the forest

as real innovators know, the only way to create real change is to take risks, and with those risks often comes the potential for failure. Being under the spotlight can magnify failures and make innovators more risk-averse—influencing their ability to create the type of disruption needed for real change. When a person's role is declared as 'the innovator,' he or she is going to be taking risks under the spotlight. That is daunting, even for the best and more seasoned among us.

Consciously or not, it will hold back the quality of the creative thinking that is being asked for. Although 'innovation' has become an increasingly popular buzzword, the overwhelming majority of people maintain a strong, innate bias against new ideas—paradoxically, even those ideas they claim to want. For a work to be truly creative, for an idea to explore its potential and reach, it has to depart from the norm and push beyond the boundaries of the known and proven; that very departure makes many people uneasy. Objective evidence shoring up the validity of a creative proposal does not motivate or condition people to accept it. If you are a practicing designer or consultant, you've witnessed your clients dismiss creative ideas in favor of ideas that are purely practical—tried and true.

For example, in a Cornell University Social and Behavioural Sciences studies[18], participants expressed a negative reaction to a running shoe equipped with nanotechnology that adjusted fabric thickness to cool the runner's foot while reducing the conditions that create blisters because of friction. To uncover bias against creativity, the researchers used a subtle technique to measure unconscious bias—the kind to which people may not want to admit, such as racism. Results revealed that while people explicitly claimed to desire creative ideas, they actually associated creative ideas with negative

---

[18] news.cornell.edu/stories/2011/08/people-are-biased-against-creative-ideas-studies-find

words such as "vomit," "poison," and "agony." These associations play up the bias that causes subjects to reject novel, high-quality ideas for new products. These findings imply a deep irony. Uncertainty drives the search for and generation of new and creative ideas, but uncertainty also makes us less able to recognize creativity, even when we need it most.

Revealing the existence and nature of a bias against creativity can help explain why people might reject creative ideas and stifle scientific advancements, even in the face of strong intentions to the contrary. The field of creativity may need to shift its current focus from identifying how to generate more creative ideas to identify how to help innovative institutions recognize and accept creativity.

Anti-creativity bias is so subtle that people are unaware of it, which can interfere with their ability to recognize a creative idea. The next time your great idea at work elicits silence or eye rolls, you might just have experienced that anti-creativity bias. Research indicates people don't even know what a creative idea looks like and that creativity, hailed as a positive change agent, actually makes people squirm. How is it that people say they want creativity but in reality often reject it? This initiates tension between failure or incompetence; when people reject a creative idea, did the idea fail? Or are those evaluating it incompetent? Did the originator(s) of the idea fail in their positioning and storytelling, or did this happen out of incompetence?

Speak to any designer or consultant, especially if they are still making their way into the discipline of innovation, and they will share that the inner battle that rages on in their minds and guts is the constant questioning, the relentless balancing whether their thoughts are good enough, competent enough, to be expressed. Or,

05 The trees and the forest

if these will be labeled or result in failure. Because of being under that spotlight, carrying the weight of having the right answers and ideas, creative people are often merciless self-critics to begin with. Our identity is tied closely with our ideas and how these are received either builds us up or tear us down if we let that happen.

Let's face it, many people have the attitude, "If it ain't broke, don't fix it." I've once heard a manager use that as a reason to reject insight-based creativity. To which I quipped that my role in the project is that "If it ain't broke, perhaps I need to hit it harder." Jokes aside, these people will rarely ever understand the need for change or why their bosses even needed to hire someone to that end. Innovative ideas can displace colleagues, potentially jeopardize their jobs or title, or at the other spectrum, create more work for them. Not everyone is adaptable in the workplace and this fear can cause distrust, or negative perceptions, of those identified as the "innovators." We then end up having permission to do everything but the ability to do nothing.

Our practice has made Design-Thinking our go-to move—wanted to make sure the right problem is defined before we unleash our expertise toward solving it. Designers, like myself, act a little like an anthropologist to understand human needs and problems before jumping to solutions. If you're anything like me, you delay the converging as long as the project can tolerate it, and you may even have my habit of not even using the term 'solution.' Instead, I describe these as 'possibilities.' Whatever is labeled a solution today, is tomorrow's design problem. To condition the right expectations and mindset, using the term 'possibility' over 'solution' has proven, for me, to soften the tensions around failure/incompetence. Both for myself and for the teams involved. But it has not yet helped those outside of the practice of creativity and advice to let go of the need

Counterintuitivity · making meaningful innovation

to have validation for new ideas before approving them. Most of those in business, if they need to embrace how to do something new, need "the illusion of rationality." For the innovation initiative to move forward, this round of irrelevance is a waste of time and resources—yet one that keeps a lot of people occupied, as I learned firsthand.

Ultimately, while basic design and creative methods can be learned much like muscles, and developed and strengthened through practice, this shift in mindset requires a different kind of leadership. It necessitates a new breed of leader who has developed and can use both sides of the brain—linear analysis for planning and executing when the decision-making information is known, and a discovery mindset for using small bets to create the data. I will wear my bias on my sleeve here because for me, this is a role that a designer-at-heart is perfectly suited for. Our role is to embody the culture that is conducive to any playbook of innovation.

Such a culture is not only good for a company's bottom line, it is also something that both leaders and employees value in their organizations. During projects at companies across the world and regardless of industry or market, I've often informally surveyed dozens of managers about whether they want to work in a way that will see innovative behaviors as the norm. Creative, open-minded thinking, the exploration of ideas. I cannot think of a single instance when someone has said, "No, I don't."

05 The trees and the forest

Part 2
Questioning the questions

"we have to continually
be jumping off cliffs
and developing our wings
on the way down."

—Kurt Vonnegut, Writer

Counterintuitivity · making meaningful innovation

PART 2 • QUESTIONING THE QUESTIONS

chapter 6
You Call That Innovation?

OVER THE DECADES, innovations have happened across industries, in waves that ripple out across global economies. The recent wave of innovation has been in apps. At the core of it, an app is an attempt to apply a market into our household lives. Facilitating buyers and sellers to convene for the sale of goods or services, hosted in virtual spaces where people meet to buy or sell. Just like they would on a market square. Uber, Airbnb, Spotify, Amazon, and so on are all pocket-sized markets. Maybe that description feels unfamiliar—because we're used to "markets" being financial or demographic. But apps are markets, too—for taxis, lodging, songs, household help, ads, personal data, basic consumer goods, and so on. The objective of innovation for these kinds of markets is by and large the "algorithmatization" of personal, yet anonymous, market exchanges of even the tiniest of everyday human interactions. Data to inform new patterns that reinforce the former ones. Forming, in essence, one exponentially growing algorithmic market that is currently inundating families, communities, towns, schools, government, social, and cultural structures. What a market creates is efficiencies. That's

06 You call that innovation?

its upside: convenience, ease, familiarity, repeatability. But there are downsides to markets. Markets erode trust, amplify inequality, and push the cost and risk to the least empowered. That is why, today, societies are reacting so explosively against globalization: trade deals broke trust, failed to bridge middle classes, and average workers lost jobs and income.

Apps, and the devices hosting them, now define our modern world. The big, educated, industrialized, rich and (mostly) democratized economies, where you'd expect life to be better for those living there are precisely where living standards are in retreat. In some of these established economies, like the US, life expectancy has actually fallen by two years. There appears a pattern that developing economies who grow past their initial renaissance suddenly see a rise in living expenses, a divide in communities, an erosion of trust, and an overall sense of unhappiness.

I've seen that first hand in China, where the economic 'wonder' of the first decade of the century saw a rise in obesity, a more visible divide between income classes, an accelerated pollution problem, all while the cost of living goes up. I see that pattern repeating in Vietnam, Laos, and Indonesia. The better we have it technologically, the worse we feel seem to feel about what it does for us. If this is what is happening in both developed, innovative societies, such as the US and the UK, and the ones that are striving to be, the inescapable conclusion I make is that innovation simply isn't working. Not any more, not the way it once did. And certainly not how we are billing it to be. The most that innovation does today is either mitigate or fuel the regress in living quality standards of our now digitally-led world.

Counterintuitivity · making meaningful innovation

I will say this again; innovation—especially in apps—is not living up to its billing, nor to the promise we housed in it. That may rub you the wrong way. At first, when this insight surfaced, it did that for me. Being myself a designer whose days are spent in delivering innovation programs, working with professionals in the innovation disciplines, I looked for ways out of this logic. I was chained to the notion of innovation being about the betterment of humanity. My sense of self is defined by this notion that I design for good, and I defend this with all my energy. But once I took the courageous action to shift perspective and see things detached from ego and assumption, I am seeing that innovation is failing us. Right here, in my pocket, is a device that can summon food, cars, and millions of other consumer goods to my door. I can talk with everyone I've ever met, create and store a photographic record of my entire life, and tap into the entire corpus of human knowledge with a few swipes. Steve Jobs wasn't exaggerating when, in 2007, he described the iPhone as a kind of magical object[19]. But in the span of a few years, we've managed to turn these talismanic tools into stress-inducing albatrosses.

Now, I am not writing this book to decimate innovation, stop doing it, or make it go away. I want, in fact, to defend it. Reposition it such that, with a deeper understanding, more possibilities are emerging to make ideas happen. Ideas that can hold innovation to its promise and bring new meanings and experiences that enrich our lives. Because if innovation doesn't, then soon more people will revolt against it. In much the same way as they have always revolted against things that have failed to deliver on the promise of a better life. And how today democracy, globalization, and capitalism are met with rising displeasure because of a sense of a promise broken.

Our app markets and the innovations we introduce through them are prone to the same incendiary failings of globalization.

[19] BBC News, 9 Jan 2007 http://news.bbc.co.uk/2/hi/technology/6246063.stm

06 You call that innovation?

That's not a coincidence—both are markets, ignoring their very real downsides; erosion of trust, expansion of inequality, pushing risk and cost to those least empowered. People are aware and mindful about the data that is harvested from them. We almost relate to it as if like gravity; we know that it's there, it's all around us, and no one can escape it. When we visualize this data capturing action, we think of cameras and 'big brother.' When in reality, we allow ourselves to be surveilled simply because we use technology. From mobile phones to cashless payment transactions, to any click or load on a browser; every technology enabled connected device gathers data. For a case study to back that claim up, look no further than Facebook's 2018, when the U.K. parliament[20] released a set of internal Facebook emails, it revealed what was really going on.

The big year for Facebook was 2012. In April of that year, Facebook announced it would acquire Instagram and, in October, FB announced it had one billion active monthly users. One in seven humans was an active Facebooker. "Helping a billion people connect is amazing, humbling, and by far the thing I am most proud of in my life," Mark Zuckerberg wrote then in a public post, announcing the milestone. "I am committed to working every day to make Facebook better for you, and hopefully together we will be able to connect the rest of the world, too." In another post that day, Zuckerberg wrote that he and his colleagues at Facebook "believe that the need to open up and connect is what makes us human. It's what brings us together. It's what brings meaning to our lives." From the released emails, however, we know now that just weeks after they hit their billionth active monthly user milestone, Zuckerberg sent an email to his colleagues with his thoughts on the data access terms and conditions that Facebook should want for any other app that operates on its platform.

---

[20] Wall Street Journal, 5 Dec 2018 https://www.wsj.com/articles/u-k-releases-internal-facebook-emails-deliberating-data-access-1544022496

"I think we should go with full reciprocity and access to app friends for no charge. Full reciprocity means that apps are required to give any user who connects to FB a prominent option to share all of their social content within that service back to Facebook," Zuckerberg wrote. "We're trying to enable people to share everything they want, and to do it on Facebook. Sometimes the best way to enable people to share something is to have a developer build a special purpose app or network for that type of content and to make that app social by having Facebook plug into it. However, that may be good for the world, but it's not good for us unless people also share back to Facebook and that content increases the value of our network."

Zuckerberg was describing the terms Facebook sets for third-party apps built on its platform. The arrangement determines how much, and which kinds, of data Facebook requires those apps to provide in return for access to its network. In this case, apps were given access to friend lists. With data gathered through reciprocity, Facebook's advertisers would be able to target users even better than before. I want to mention that Facebook says the exposed email had been "cherry-picked," and that it "tells only one side of the story and omits important context." FB suggested that this email was not a directive, but merely an internal conversation or exploration of all possibilities.

In other emails, Zuckerberg did discuss user data in a different context: how it might be obtained by another party. In an email[21] to then-VP of product management, Sam Lessin, Zuckerberg wrote that he was skeptical about any potential "data leak strategic risk," adding: "I agree there is a clear risk on the advertiser side, but I haven't figured out how that connects to the rest of the platform.

---

[21] The Guardian, 5 Dec 2018 https://www.theguardian.com/technology/2018/dec/05/facebook-emails-analysis-user-data-parliament

06 You call that innovation?

I think we leak info to developers, but I just can't think of any instances where that data has leaked from developer to developer and caused a real issue for us. Do you have examples of this?" In 2018, following the Cambridge Analytica allegations, that question now seems pretty ominous. In fairness, the offensiveness of the data privacy scandals is not that Facebook is not allowed to find ways to maximize its profits.

That's called "keeping the lights on," I get that. These emails, however, reveal a core dissonance between the idea Facebook sought to market to its now billion-plus users for years, and how those users were leveraged in a business sense. The deal Facebook users thought they were making with the site, as Zuckerberg gushed when it reached its billion-user milestone, was a provocatively yet wonderfully idealistic one. By handing over some obvious personal data to Facebook, the social site would provide, in return, a form of unprecedented global connection that would provide things like fulfilment and deeper meaning.

That ultimately proved to be deceiving. Facebook's utopian language also implied that the arrangement users had committed to by signing up for the platform—using their personal data as entry—was not merely reciprocal, but equal. It is not and never was. To believe there's any kind of equal exchange in Facebook's relationships with either its users or app developers (not to mention media companies) would be a mistake.

As we've come to discover, equal partnerships are not what has helped Facebook succeed; instead, Facebook thrives on inequality. The platform is built on a fundamental imbalance of power between itself and its users. Because, ultimately, Facebook has benefited a lot more than its users have. Strictly financially, some of those benefits

Counterintuitivity · making meaningful innovation

are obvious. Facebook, along with Google, now controls around 50% of online advertising spending, is worth about $630 billion, and the site has made Mark Zuckerberg one of the richest people on Earth. But beyond those staggering figures, Facebook has benefited in other ways, too, not least of which is that it's become an assumed part of life in many countries around the world. The Cambridge Analytica allegations shook the company to its core, and the brand paid a steep price for it. A delayed reaction by Zuckerberg would suggest the brand was a victim itself, and that this was—at worse—an isolated event.

An anomaly. Mark apologized, playing up a vulnerability of having meant no harm, and doing it all out of innocence. Thankfully, it prompted deeper investigations and questioning which soon placed the company in an even worse light. Early December 2018, during an interview, Facebook's VP of marketing solutions, Carolyn Everson[22], explained to a reporter, "We care deeply, as deep as a company can care about privacy. It's the foundation of our company, and we want people to know that we care." A few days later the company copped to a bug that gave app developers access to private user photos, which raised quite a few eyebrows. Then on December 18, the New York Times[23] dropped a bombshell of a story describing just how false Everson's statement was.

This article exposed details of the partnership arrangements Facebook has had with some of the largest tech companies in the world, and the clusters of user data provided to them. The records show that Facebook allowed Microsoft's Bing search engine to see the names of virtually all Facebook users' friends without consent

---

[22] DigiDay UK 13 Dec 2018 https://digiday.com/social/facebooks-carolyn-everson-privacy-foundation-company/
[23] New York Times 18 Dec 2018 https://www.nytimes.com/2018/12/18/technology/facebook-privacy.html

06 You call that innovation?

and gave Netflix and Spotify the ability to read Facebook users' private messages. Those are just a few examples; the Times says more than 150 companies had similar partnerships with Facebook, including Huawei and the Royal Bank of Canada. This revelation, along with all the details we've already learned since the Cambridge Analytica debacle, evidences the three things Facebook really cares about: user data, growth, and how the two together further the company's wealth.

As a mere "platform" for "sharing," Facebook sells itself as a neutral, even fair, player. We now know that it is not. It poetically reasons to do all this because they care about us, but that is getting harder and harder to believe. Facebook's assimilation into every corner of our lives has indeed made some aspects of life better. It's easy, for instance, to communicate with friends, join groups of like-minded people, or even shop. But at every turn, Facebook tips the scales in its favor. It hunts for more ways to gather data, create a wider network, and push for more engagement. It actively seeks to create and dominate new markets and to exploit those that already exist. Along the way, it has undermined the fabric of communities and destabilized civil society. Reported by Reuters[24] and the BBC[25], U.N. human rights experts investigating a possible genocide in Myanmar said that Facebook had played a role in spreading hate speech there. Nevertheless, Facebook got its data all the same. For a lot of us, we've finally reached "peak Facebook." People are becoming aware that the platform hurts society, not necessarily as a side effect. Facebook is an intentionally bad actor.

Mind you, FB is not the only actor in this play. There is Uber[26], who reduced trust overall in society. Lowering the bar for what is

---

[24] Reuters 15 Aug 2018 https://www.reuters.com/investigates/special-report/myanmar-facebook-hate/
[25] BBC 12 Sep 2018 https://www.bbc.com/news/blogs-trending-45449938

acceptable behavior by a CEO and a corporation, constantly attacking norms and laws. As hip as they portray themselves to be, risks and costs are shifted to drivers (and as such back to society) as a driver is not quite an employee, and as such things like insurance, healthcare, safety regulation, and so on; none is provided. Meanwhile, these drivers are not entrepreneurs either, so other than a handout, there is nothing much in it for them. That model gets copied into firms like Grab[27], the Uber equivalent in South East Asia. Here, too, creating sets of winners and losers; where management and shareholders have become super-rich, but the average driver has shared less than nothing in those gains—his real income, like that of the average American, is shrinking—and so economic inequality has been reinforced.

The digital markets we innovate in, under the banner of improving lives, are not mitigating falling living standards. They are fueling the decline of them. The drive and hunger for tech innovation are creating a new kind of caste society; owners of digital capital and creators of data patterns to condition people to obey the algorithm faster and harder than the previous version. What these app markets are replicating is the economic model of domination. For centuries, countries and corporations made their fortunes and gained their respect by dominating all others. What they couldn't dominate, they exploited. Should we call that innovation?

These algorithm-driven "advances" are now dominating life in the first world, but are not optimized to provide a higher quality of life. It is only optimized for speed, scale, and profit. The costs are human, social, cultural, environmental or political collateral. Of

---

[26] The Guardian 6 Dec 2016 https://www.theguardian.com/technology/2016/dec/09/uber-drivers-report-sweated-labour-minimum-wage
[27] StraitsTimes 8 May 2018 https://www.straitstimes.com/singapore/transport/grab-cuts-user-discounts-and-driver-incentives

06 You call that innovation?

course, there are upsides to this kind of market. Convenience goes a long way. The question isn't whether the upsides outweigh the downsides, but whether these are even considered, seen or understood at all. I'm not convinced these are. I increasingly see economies asking for more innovations, so they can be run by algorithms that, just like the deals of global trade, reduce human beings to dehumanized commodities.

For innovation to be about "making lives better" that very idea must be put first. Making people's lives better means, at a minimum, solving the problems that affect them. But the last wave of innovation isn't solving any of today's great global problems: inequality, shrinking middle classes, climate change, extremism, authoritarianism, loneliness, distrust. Increasingly, as the product and services we innovate to be inherently connected, and as we infuse these with social elements, the decision to opt in or out of a product or service becomes a decision for you to opt in or out of the society you live in. Said differently, increasing our efforts to innovate in the "Me, Myself and AI" era is carving a divisional line between inclusion, opting in, or exclusion, opting out. That which divides people, or leaves them behind, should not be called innovation.

Counterintuitivity · making meaningful innovation

PART 2 • QUESTIONING THE QUESTIONS

chapter 7
Does One Size Fit All?

IT'S THE WORD that a lot of us would tend to cleverly wiggle our way out of having to explain: "innovation." Most of the time, those asked will be tempted to reply with something like "new stuff," or "clever idea no-one else thought of." The more versed in the subject, often those who are actively pursuing it, would likely state that innovation is "that which makes people's lives better." But if that is what we are benchmarking it to then, by and large, innovation tends to fall rather short of that mark. Why isn't innovation doing precisely that which we want it to do? There are distinctions to the term that may help deepen our understanding that innovation is not a one-size offer.

I will say this again; innovation is not living up to its billing, nor to the promise we housed in it. That may rub you the wrong way. At first, when this insight surfaced, it did that for me. Being myself a designer whose days are spent in delivering innovation programs, working with professionals in the innovation disciplines, I looked for ways out of this logic. I was chained to the notion of innovation

07 Does one size fit all?

being about the betterment of humanity. My sense of self is defined by this notion that I design for good, and I defend this with all my energy. But once I took the courageous action to shift perspective and see things detached from ego and assumption, I am seeing that innovation is failing us.

Now, I am not writing this book to decimate innovation, to have us stop doing it, or to make it go away. I want, in fact, to defend it. Reposition it such that, with a deeper understanding, more possibilities are emerging to make ideas happen. Ideas that can hold innovation to its promise and have it bring new meanings and experiences that enrich our lives. Because if innovation doesn't, then soon more people will revolt against it. In much the same way as they have always revolted against things that have failed to deliver on the promise of a better life. And how today democracy, globalization, and capitalism are met with rising displeasure because of a sense of a promise broken.

What can be done to fix the shortfall of innovation? How can we innovate or be an innovator in a device-led, online, data-driven world? The following takes a beginner's mind to present different perspectives for you-the-reader to consider. I'm not aiming to be argumentative, but I may be provocative. There is no agenda to prove anyone right or wrong, it is an invitation to reflect on your/the act of innovation as if you are, once more, a blank slate to it. Before you can be anything else, you have to dare to be a beginner first. And beginners ask questions. I am inviting you to park aside your knowledge so that curiosity can pose the question "What should we call innovation?"

No doubt the term innovation is bankrupt for some of us, particularly those who throw the word around without defining it clearly. I can offer a simple, five-word definition: "Something different that has impact." I know it doesn't nail down much of anything, but this is kept intentionally broad to help disarm three common misconceptions.

The first misconception is that innovation and creativity are the same things that both result in the same outcome. Those who fall into this trap think that the best way to solve the innovation problem is to bring in a wide range of right-brained thinkers, put them in a room, and ask them to think of awesome ideas. There is no doubt that awesome ideas serve as an important input that can lead to impact, but if you stop at idea-generation, you are destined to suffer disappointing results.

When most organizations try to increase their innovation efforts, they always seem to start from the same assumption: "We need more ideas." They'll start talking about the need to "think outside the box" or "blue sky" thinking in order to find a few ideas that can turn into viable new products or systems. It's believed that the most difficult thing is to find is a new idea, however, once we have a great one put in front of us, it can be easily recognized, even if introduced by outsiders. Practical for when innovating solutions, since solutions can be, more or less easily, judged by how well these enable us to solve the given problem. Be that the case, in most organizations, I would say innovation isn't hampered by a lack of ideas, but rather a lack of noticing the good ideas. It's not an idea problem; it's a recognition problem. Innovation is a design process. One that could potentially combine discovering an opportunity, blueprinting an idea to seize that opportunity, and implementing that idea to achieve results. That is but one way of innovating something with meaning, which should be the overall aim—no impact, no innovation.

07 Does one size fit all?

A second common misconception is that only a select group of people should drive a company's innovation activities. Only specialists need to apply, only they will have the privilege to define new meaning bestowed upon them. It's this pop culture visual that innovation lives in labs, and it is done by white-lab-coated nerds. However, since design is a human capability, everyone in an organization can—and should—think about doing something different that has an impact. Not all innovations come in the same flavor, of course.

The third misconception is that innovation is all about "shazaam." A head-turner moment. The next iPod-iPad-iPhone. The pursuit for the universe's next big bang often leads to overly risky ideas that have little hope of getting approved at most companies. The innovation scoreboard is measured not in the size of the vision, the beauty of the financial forecasts, or the degree of difficulty made redundant, but in what meaning the act has, or better still, what new meaning it is introducing.

Now that this is clarified, back to the question; what do I call innovation? Not as something sexy and mysterious. Not as a helpful bromide to a struggling organization. Certainly as something energizing, and, when managed properly, with world-changing impact. Above all, innovation—for me—is a discipline to be nurtured and managed. It is hard work. Getting good at it requires significant practice.

I build on the framework of professor Clayton Christensen, who, in his book The Innovator's Dilemma[28], defined three categories of innovation. I am taking the initiative to introduce a fourth. These four playbooks (as I call them) stretch along a continuum of what is known, and can be iterated upon to be re-experienced as 'more-

---

[28] https://www.amazon.com/Innovators-Dilemma-Technologies-Management-Innovation-ebook/dp/B012BLTM6I

better,' to what is unknown; what needs to be defined, created, and experienced for the first time. The four kinds of innovation playbooks (fig.4) are; 'keep the momentum,' 'making a breakthrough,' 'creating a disruption,' and—my addition—'forging new paths.'

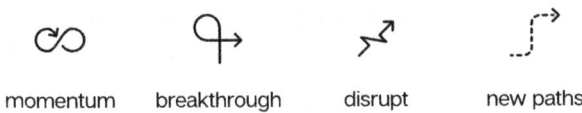

fig.4 The four playbooks of innovation

Most innovations happen by the 'keep the momentum' playbook, because most of the time we are seeking to get better at what we're already doing, we have a pretty clear idea of what problems need to be solved and what skill domains are required to solve them. Conventional methods like strategic roadmapping, traditional R&D labs, and using acquisitions to bring new resources and skill sets into the organization are usually effective. Design-thinking can be helpful if both the problem and the skills needed to solve it are well understood. Here you can—and should—apply 'Best Practices' because when seeking to get better at what you are already doing, the criteria for best practice should be understood.

When innovation is keen to make a shift, a breakthrough, it is dealing with a well-defined problem that's just incredibly hard to solve. In cases like these, unconventional skill domains and open innovation strategies will be more effective than user-centricity or Design-Thinking only, because these will help to expose the problem to diverse skill domains. As Thomas Kuhn explained in the 'The Structure of Scientific Revolutions[29]': sometimes it will be very difficult to solve a problem within the domain in which it arose—but

[29] https://www.amazon.com/Structure-Scientific-Revolutions-Thomas-Kuhn/dp/0226458083

07 Does one size fit all?

the problem may be resolved fairly easily within the paradigm of an adjacent domain. Or in Einstein's words; new problems require new thinking. That means you'd be more realistic to benchmark 'Good Practices' for this effort, because there won't be enough certainty for what the practice needs to aim for.

When professor Clayton Christensen introduced the concept of disruptive innovation, it was a revelation. In his study of why good firms fail, he found that what is normally considered best practice—listening to customers, investing in continuous improvement, and focusing on the bottom line—will not position you to disrupt a category of industry. It will do the opposite; make you a prime target to get disrupted. The aim of an innovation act can be to disrupt. What professor Christensen introduces is that when the basis of competition changes, because of technological shifts or other changes in the marketplace, companies can find themselves getting better and better at things people want less and less. When that happens, innovating your products won't help—you have to innovate your business model. Traditional management by planning and prediction is great for tuning a machine—optimizing a business—but today's world demands a new management approach that transforms the risk of change into an asset, by supporting real entrepreneurship and venture-style investing within very large companies.

It's bringing in another exponential variable in the mix; the scale of involvement for a company in their efforts to innovate. In keeping the momentum, innovation will be a silo within the organization, possibly within a department. When making breakthroughs, innovation will need to move horizontally across a few other departments in order to achieve its goal. Disruption can only be created by an initiative that has been originated or championed by the organization's leadership.

Counterintuitivity · making meaningful innovation

Then what about that fourth playbook, 'forging new paths'? For this to occur, a company's purpose must be about creating new values, new meanings, by tackling the grander challenges. It can do this because they operate out of an established systemic innovation ecosystem, and, more importantly, they work out of a vision. One of the things I was searching for while understanding innovation was some commonality between the incredibly diverse group of innovators I came across. What could tie together this medley of extroverts, introverts, scientists, daydreamers, night thinkers, entrepreneurs, intrapreneurs, designers, and strategic executives?

What I found was that all actively seek out new problems to solve. In other words, they not only continue to hone their existing processes and practices, they go actively look for areas where they can make an impact. These are, by definition, highly speculative and hard to predict, with lots of blind alleys and wrong turns, but they pay off in the end. To be successful, this innovation effort needs to include capabilities to help entrepreneurs and business leaders launch new ventures. A deep collaboration with different partners to confidently identify opportunities unseen, and likely not yet understood by others, develop solutions for these, and build the infrastructure required to launch new products, services, and businesses into the market. The most important type of problem for creating long-term value is a grand challenge, a new possibility. These can be a new experience type of proposition, or sustainable, long-term efforts to solve a fundamental problem. Their impact is not measured in weeks or months, but years and decades. New path innovations never arrive fully formed because there is no case study or previous model that can determine a required state. They almost always begin with a discovery of some new phenomenon or technology. Bringing to fruition the ideas or opportunities in the mind of an innovator. It comes with emergence and uncertainties. No one could

07 Does one size fit all?

guess how Einstein's discoveries would shape the world we know today, or that Alan Turing's room-sized contraption would someday become a consumer commodity.

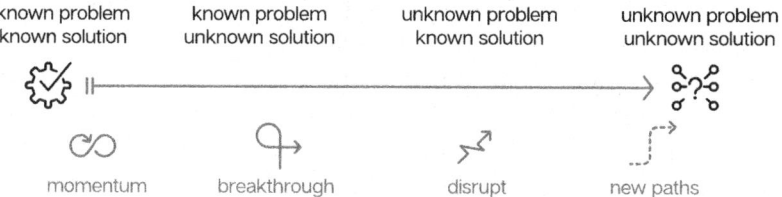

fig.5 The four playbooks of innovation in their problem space continuum

Going from left to right on the continuum (fig.5), from known and defined, to unknown and undefined, spans the boundaries between innovating and inventing. The less known and defined, the more our imagination needs to be willing to explore. The stronger our vision needs to become. In keeping a momentum, innovators look outside to find ideas to solve a known condition. Design-Thinking and user-centricity will get you where you need to end up. It fits the nature of solutions.

When the aim is to forge new paths, when the ambition is to define new values, you aim for innovation of meaning. Meanings have a different nature than solutions. New meanings will need new interpretations of what is good and what is bad. There won't be a scale of judgment because what we innovate is the scale of the judgment itself. Proposing new meanings and new interpretations are relatively straight forward, and by unleashing our imagination, we will soon see a world full of opportunities. What is difficult instead is understanding which of them actually makes sense. That won't be made evident by asking those we call 'users,' nor by squeezing the potential out of last week's new feature.

Counterintuitivity · making meaningful innovation

"We never see any good ideas," lamented a senior executive. "Our people bring us ideas all the time. But they just don't have any... magic." At first, I found the comment surprising. I had just begun to get to know the company, and it seemed to me to be brimming with innovation energy; the department was declared the brand's Innovation Center. Among product teams where someone would regularly throw out creative "What if's" during casual conversations. Others offered targeted and well-grounded strategies and frameworks to what idea could work in what market, for which demographic.

Soon, it was clear that the problem—as is almost always the case—wasn't a lack of raw ideas. Instead, there was a problem with the process that an idea generator had to go through before they stood in front of senior leadership. The innovation team, it turned out, had a deep case of missing the wood from the forest. Anything that was considered to go onto the agenda of the top management's biweekly meeting was vetted. And screened. And debated. And reformulated. The idea generator had to show the idea to their line manager. Get buy-ins from key functional representatives. Appeal to staff members of senior leadership. Maybe even requiring the sponsorship of one or two members of this leadership. Every person who saw the idea would express a clear point of view, and the idea lead would then figure out how to integrate seemingly contradictory feedback. By the time he or she had gone through this gauntlet of gatekeepers, the ideas became watered down and wafer-thin—acceptable to everyone, exciting to no one.

Should we call that innovation? The newness or differentiating is iterated right out of the initial spark before it had a chance to ignite anything. That's not to say that those that generate ideas shouldn't get feedback. They should. But too much feedback too early transforms formerly interesting ideas into well-documented

07 Does one size fit all?

bowls of 'meh.' Is the innovation community in danger of becoming unable to innovate itself? Are the innovation evangelists locked into incremental thinking—just like the corporations they are advising to change?

Innovation—regardless of the which of the four playbooks it is running—calls us to do the impossible: to build for a future we can't yet see. The very notion of innovation is riddled with paradoxes. It asks us to embrace wildly different—even contradictory—approaches at once: creativity and pragmatism, foresight and hindsight, breakthrough visions and incremental change. In this way, innovation is unlike all the other design or business things we do on an everyday basis. The murkiness happens when these businesses spend too much time thinking outside the box without first redefining what that box is going to be; are we keeping the momentum of a previous initiative and improving on it? Do we adapt to the market needs and make a breakthrough offer? Are we setting out to disrupt our, or a parallel, category? Or do we seek an entirely new proposition that introduces new meaning, new experiences, and new expressions?

Each of the innovation playbooks requires their own unique set of skills, and the more meaningful the innovation, the more emergent these skill-sets need to be. Across all these scenarios, there are three defining characteristics that differentiate innovation from all other forms of value. The first is its time-based nature. Innovation happens in the future for which we have no data now. It can only be a future if it is unclear and undefined. We can't predict the future, but we can prepare for it, and predictions or patterns can help forecast what tomorrow may look and feel like. The other complication to innovation's time-based character is its inevitable expiration date: innovation has a shelf life. It goes sour like milk. An innovation doesn't stay an innovation for very long—regardless of the impact

Counterintuitivity · making meaningful innovation

it created. If your efforts are incremental, the turnaround cycle can be as short as a two-week sprint. With the recognition and sense of reward from users as short as a moment.

The second key quality of innovation is positive deviance. What makes an innovation valuable is the amount of divergence it allows for from the standard or accepted norms. In all other situations, when we plan for something, we assume that there will be continuity between today and tomorrow. The opposite is—should be—true for innovation, where we seek out and depend on discontinuity. This quality can be important when looking for a breakthrough, will need to be prevalent in disruptive innovation, and imperative when forging new paths. Just take a look at Tesla Motors. Everything about the company is disruptively deviant—the way its cars look, the way it sells its cars online without a showroom, the way it makes cars from stock parts you can get from any supplier. The only thing that's not out of the norm about Tesla is the individual pieces of technology it uses. It is what we usually assume as the most innovative thing a cutting-edge organization like Tesla would be doing—creating new technology. But it doesn't do anything out of standard here. Meaning, the brand is deviant in both its process and in the very way it conceives of what it calls innovation.

A last, third element to take into consideration of determining what to call innovation is that happens (read: should happen) horizontally. Typically, organizations strive for alignment at a leadership level, working to make sure that all the key performance indicators (KPI's), line up nicely and that all departments are on the same page. And then cascade those performance metrics down the chain. With the possible exception of the momentum kind, in innovation, things don't work that way. That's because for innovation to be meaningful and of impacting potential, it needs to cut across all

07 Does one size fit all?

the boundaries and disciplines of a business practice. When it cannot reach across departmental silos, often there's only one element of a product ecosystem that has an element of innovation. It could be in the packaging, like it is for Procter & Gamble's Air Assist[30], a breakthrough in performance and sustainability for e-commerce and retail packaging that uses 50% less plastic than a traditional rigid bottle and has a 360-degree palette for design, making it a more resource-efficient solution. It could be in customer service, like it is for Singapore Airlines, where the brand leverages its service reputation as its signature innovation. It could be in the distribution process, like it is for Federal Express, who introduced a redistribution retail offer for the used cardboard boxes. Sold on markets, out of the back of a Fedex van, under a marquee tent. For brands with a heritage and legacy, the challenge is in bringing out a single innovative aspect of an idea while maintaining the contributions, support and voice from all other sectors.

Our conventional strategies or consulting practices, like Design-Thinking or brand strategy, would tackle such friction points with alignment. But innovation should resist alignment and require synchronization instead. Alignment waters down, compromises, brushes over, dulls out. Alignment seeks the straight and narrow. Innovators don't want straight lines—we just want everything to go together at the right time. This is not unlike an orchestra where everyone is playing a different instrument and different parts, but they're all playing the same piece of music.

---

[30] https://corporate.dow.com/en-us/news/press-releases/procter--gamble-earns-top-honors-in-dows-2018-30th-awards-for-packaging-innovation

Counterintuitivity · making meaningful innovation

PART 2 • QUESTIONING THE QUESTIONS

chapter 8
Is It Only The Lucky Few?

CREATIVITY HAS MOVED up in the world—where it used to be a nice-to-have, increasingly it is becoming a must-have. I consider it among the most critical characteristics of modern leadership, among the highest forms of self-actualization and learning. Creativity drives our innovations and the growth we seek to get from them. Having a creative disposition is no longer 'that extra little thing' you may be able to offer. It is not a good-on-you thing; instead, it is a 21st century survival skill.

There seems to be wide support for the idea that this century is an "age of complexity," which implies that the world has never been more intricate. With the rapid pace of technological changes, and the vast amount of information that we are generating—the two are related—it feels like it is a recent phenomenon. Consider philosophers like Leibniz (17th century) and Diderot (18th century) who were complaining about information overload in their lifetimes. What they depict as the "horrible mass of books" would only represent a fraction of what all we know today, but much of what we know

08 Is it only the lucky few?

today will be equally insignificant to our future generations. Regardless, the complexity of different eras is of little matter to the person who is overwhelmed by it today. The question to ask is not "Is this era more complex?" but rather, "Why are some people more able to manage complexity?" Certainly, complexity is context-dependent, but it is also determined by a person's disposition. There are three key qualities that enhance our ability to manage complexity in the quest for innovation: IQ, EQ, and increasingly, the need for a CQ.

As most people know, IQ stands for Intelligence Quotient and refers to a person's mental ability. Now, recently, IQ has been getting a bit of shade, as if it is not all that important anymore. The fact, however, is that IQ does affect a wide range of real-world outcomes. The higher the levels of someone's IQ, the more enabled and faster their learning and complex problem-solving capabilities. Sure, at a glance, IQ tests seem rather abstract and disconnected from everyday life problems. However, they are a powerful tool to predict our ability to manage complexity. In fact, complex environments are richer in information, which creates more cognitive load and demands more brain-power or deliberate thinking from us. IQ is a measure of that brainpower, just like megabytes or processing speed are a measure of the operations a computer can perform, and at what speed.

What gets more attention, and perhaps even priority, is EQ; Emotional Quotient. Indicating our ability and awareness in perceiving, managing, and expressing emotions. EQ relates to complexity management in three main ways. First, individuals with higher EQ benefit from being aware and more mindful in that they are less susceptible to stress and anxiety. Since complex situations are emotionally demanding, they tend to increase feelings of pressure and stress. The higher one's EQ, the bigger the buffer. People with higher EQs are better equipped to navigate complex organizational politics, thanks to their more developed interpersonal skills—the second way it helps to manage innovation's complexity. Even in today's hyper-connected world, what most employers now prioritize is less the technical expertise, but much more the soft skills, or 'people skills.' For management and leadership roles, these are now imperative. Third, and lastly, those empowered with higher EQ dare to be more entrepreneurial. Being more proactive at exploiting opportunities, taking risks, and turning creative ideas into actual innovations. All this makes EQ an important quality for adapting to uncertain, unpredictable, and complex environments.

There is a third quotient that is required to be a successful contributor to the innovation act. The Creativity Quotient, or CQ, consists of a more inquisitive mind that is both open to and able to imagine new experiences. These are individuals who find novelty exciting and are quickly bored with routine. They tend to generate an abundance of original ideas and are counter-conformist. I suggest it is just as important when it comes to managing complexity in the quest for innovation. First, individuals with higher CQ are much more tolerant of ambiguity. In fact they revel in it as it liberates their thinking and curiosity. This nuanced, sophisticated, subtle thinking defines the very essence of the complexity that is present in the disruptive and new path play-books of innovation. Then, CQ leads to higher levels of intellectual and knowledge acquisition over time. Knowledge and expertise, much like experience, translate complex situations into familiar ones, so CQ is what produces those seemingly simple solutions for complex, wicked problems.

It is a falsehood to state that you lack creativity. Whether it's at work, or through hobbies, or simply in the way we live, we are always expressing fragments of who we are. A big part of living a fulfilling life is doing so in a way that is true. An expression is a physi-

08 Is it only the lucky few?

cal form we give to a part of ourselves, and it's ultimately what connects us to the outer world. In the smallest of our acts and action, creativity is present. If the act of design requires creativity, then, as defended in earlier chapters, each of us has both the capacity and the ability to tap into our innate creative potential.

Although IQ is hard to coach or improve upon, EQ can be trained and developed, and CQ can be nurtured and grown. The seemingly unquestionable assertion that creativity is only the blessing of those lucky few geniuses does not hold up. That it requires formal artistic training or talent is only partially enabling it. Whether you are a practiced design professional or an Uber driver; you both have an abundant potential for human creativity. For starters, creativity emerges from seeing. Steve Jobs—it wouldn't be a book about innovation without drawing lessons from him—shared in an interview[31] that, "Creativity is just connecting things. When you ask creative people how they did something, they feel a little guilty because they didn't really do it, they just saw something. It seemed obvious to them after a while."

This prompts me to bring in another quote; "You don't need eyes to see. You need vision." It's a line of Faithless' "Reverence" song, and it captures the narrative I want to bring next. You can be looking at things, but do you see them? Recall how, in Chapter One, I shared how successful redesigns of ordinary objects often allows us to see them again with a new understanding. Can you observe with a genuine curiosity? It may have killed the cat, but it is curiosity that sparks and then fuels creativity within us.

When I became a father, I had several re-introductions with my sense of curiosity. Everything about my daily life was now new and

---

[31] February 1995 Wired article, see https://unicheck.com/blog/steve-jobs-creativity-is-just-connecting-things

Counterintuitivity · making meaningful innovation

different, and it didn't come with instructions—just a lot of well intended opinions. As my son is growing, he displays that abundance of curiosity for e.v.e.r.y.t.h.i.n.g. Curiosity is naturally coursing through his developing mind, excitedly exploring new experiences, different possibilities, and investigating those taken-for-granted truths.

In that respect, Albert Einstein stated that he "has no special talents, apart from being passionately curious." Come to think of it, Einstein inspired a paradigm shift in physics not as a scientist, but truly as a creative. For most of us, designers and innovators included, lose this natural sense of novelty and exploration. We have to be reminded to activate curiosity and bypass certainty, security, and a simple way of making sense of the world. For innovators, curiosity is a habit because it offers the ability to truly process new discoveries and turn them into concrete ideas and strategies. Ultimately, the more we allow ourselves to follow our curiosities, the more we'll be able to connect the dots and combine new possibilities with what we already think we know. Our uniquely individual past experiences, combined with an open-mindedness to observe and discover more, leads to a truly original breakthrough in creativity. Regardless of education or vocation.

What we see is not what the universe has named, but what our collective imaginations have agreed upon, and our minds have learned to label. The labels we give things may not always be perfect, but they are important. It is how we differentiate between the various elements in our reality. Our entire construct of the world depends on language. By extension, the groups we form, the teams we work in or with, the organization that employs or contracts us, the societies we live in; these are all linguistic constructs. There are many smart and knowledgeable innovators and designers, but rare-

08 Is it only the lucky few?

ly, however, do we come across those who are capable of producing ideas and work that shifts our understanding of the world, or change our behavior. That requires an entirely new way of looking, seeing, and verbalizing.

That act, I argue, is attributed more to creativity than it is to the underlying knowledge. That act is what I label as 'visionary.' This may raise an eyebrow, but believe it not, there is not as much to it as you may think. It is simply about visualizing the thinking, and that quality of thinking is largely dependent on your CQ, your own unique Creativity Quotient. Apart from becoming or remaining habitually curious, there are a few practices that can help raise your own CQ.

For starters, don't wait for inspiration, instead, move ahead. It feels counterintuitive, but it's a misconception that creativity is a synonym for inspiration. What sparks inspiration, or what turns ideas into something inspiring, works differently for different people. Once I had a few industry years under the belt, holding a senior status, and still to this day, at conferences, workshops, or studios, someone would make a request to inspire them. I struggled to answer this question for the longest time. But it did give me the opportunity to reflect and unpack this. It's easy to fall into the trap of believing that a breakthrough idea happens suddenly, that in a pixie-dust-clouded moment, inspiration strikes. And everything after that is going to fall into place.

It actually does happen very rarely, and if it does, it will never be a finished or foolproof solution. Waiting for it to occur is almost always setting yourself up for failure. Assuming inspiration will strike by command is—in my view—an act of incompetence. For it to strike, inspiration needs to find you working. Researching, looking, asking, connecting, and reconnecting. I may have killed a vibe here, but creative work is not all glamorous and opportune. Visions, and creating them, will take work. And as with any work, it requires you to show up and produce. It requires effort and needs the discipline to "be" a creative visionary. Before you "become," the practice is in dedicating moments to "being."

In 1902, Einstein took up a job at a Swiss patent office. Though his efforts were to land himself a teaching position, he had little luck in establishing himself in the academic circles. You could say that these were less than ideal circumstances for him, and that working at this place would have him in an inopportune and uninspiring place relative to his interest in physics.

However, Einstein was undeterred and elected to manage his day with a set of hours to spend on the job, and a set of hours dedicated to doing scientific work. Obviously, this required a disciplined approach. But this commitment to creation and his use of curiosity gave the world the Annus Mirabilis papers. Or what scientists call "the miracle year." These ideas and thoughts would inspire the formulation of the two fundamental theories in physics: the theory of general relativity and quantum mechanics. Had Einstein waited for the right moment, the world would not be where it is.

Let's stay with Einstein and take another lesson in. One that, years later, Steve Jobs so famously echoed when he said that creativity is 'just connecting things that seem obvious after a while.' In 1945, Einstein wrote a letter in response to a survey by a French mathematician who was trying to understand the thinking patterns of famous scientists. It can be found in Ideas and Opinions[32], a collection of Einstein's writings, and in it, he speaks about his process:

---

[32] https://www.amazon.com/Ideas-Opinions-Albert-Einstein/dp/0517884402

08 Is it only the lucky few?

"The words or the language, as they are written or spoken, do not seem to play any role in my mechanism of thought. The psychical entities which seem to serve as elements in thought are certain signs and more or less clear images which can be 'voluntarily' reproduced and combined. It is also clear that the desire to arrive finally at logically connected concepts is the emotional basis of this rather vague play with the above-mentioned elements. But taken from a psychological viewpoint, this combinatory play seems to be the essential feature in productive thought—before there is any connection with logical construction in words or other kinds of signs which can be communicated to others."

At its core, the creativity that shapes a vision is not imaged out of thin air, or seen in tea leaves, coffee grinds, or celestial signs. Visions are not abstract conceptual hallucinations; they are new combinations or connections that offer a renewed sense of the existing components of a reality that has yet to emerge. If you accept that creativity, and the visionary ideas that it produces, has the ability to establish what you see as meaningful connections between the existing parts of your reality, then it is no longer a truth that creativity is reserved for the special ones, the lucky few. It's something all of us can practice in our own unique manner. Tap into your mental inventory of what you know, mix in what you see, and connect them in the absurd ways that only you can think of.

The challenge is that it is difficult to accept the often subpar, underwhelming uncertainty of those thoughts. Nobody likes to fall short of expectations, and it's all the more daunting when it comes to creating, even if the creation is the speaking of ideas or possibilities. The result of creativity is a tangible output, like a painting, a service model, an object—or indeed a book. Creativity invites us to make our thinking visible, and putting it out there, for others to

Counterintuitivity · making meaningful innovation

question and judge. It is a lot more enjoyable if you create out of a genuine sense of learning and solving, and less about being right and bright. Creativity is imperfect. Because you are making new connections and different thoughts, there is no longer a known state of perfect for it. If it feels imperfect, then you're doing it right. When we see a great creation by someone labeled a genius, it's useful to remember that they worked on more than just that one piece. Over the course of his career, Einstein published over 300 scientific papers and about 150 non-scientific papers. An archive of his non-published work contained more than 30,000 unique documents, and he wasn't always right. In Brilliant Blunders[33], Mario Livio estimates that about 20% of Einstein's papers contain notable mistakes. The collateral that Einstein paid for thinking unconventionally was that his work was, in fact, quite imperfect.

Another obstacle to creativity is time. Ever since the Industrial Revolution, the clock has become its own deity. It tells us when we start work, when we eat, when we move, when we sleep, when we connect, when we create: when we live. Despite this rhythm and pace feeling like that is how time is experienced by us, and that a clock is the gatekeeper of our day, we have forgotten that this is not normal at all. This obsession with habits and routines that are rigidly anchored to time is relatively recent. Prior to our capitalistic society, we had metrics and devices to signal a time, sure, but time didn't control us like it does today. Of course, organizing a structure of a day into neat little packs of eight hours of work, eight hours of play, and eight hours of sleep is a society-wide advantage. It's a practical set of rules that help us do the things we need to do. In that regard, it is practical to have our collective imagination condition us to all want, accept, and expect the same construct that makes up a day; when to wake, eat, commute, work, take a break, work some more,

---

[33] https://www.amazon.com/Brilliant-Blunders-Einstein-Scientists-Understanding-ebook/dp/B008J4B40Y

08 Is it only the lucky few?

commute again, etc. At the same time, only living in an environment where this is the norm dulls inspiration and the act of creating. Inspiration has two faces: the first is a product of action, when you actually sit down to produce something, say, like a piece of writing or a piece of music; the second, the one that fuels the first, however, is born out of the freedom to explore in a nonlinear, non-timebound manner. Inspiration is an expressive manifestation of freedom; free from restrictions, judgment, pre-conditions. Inspiration not found in places with walls. Our modern world has a bias toward structure, for the mentioned reasons, but for that structure to produce something of inspiration, it needs an undefined and unconditioned space. For your vision to have an impact, and potentially shift reality, it needs an open field. With boundaries, sure, but not with borders.

So many of us ignore our innate creative being, because the act of expressing yourself is an act of differentiation, and people at different skill and competence levels differentiate themselves in various ways that don't work for everyone. It is a moment of vulnerability; when you differentiate yourself, you put your environment to a test. A test of willingness to include again. Whether it's in art, writing, thinking, music, or in a conversation, expression is a two-person game. There is the person expressing themselves and then there is the receiver who has a response to the expression. And, I imagine you nodding your head in agreement now, everyone's a critic. Good, productive criticism, of course, is vital for feedback and improvement, but only if it's coming from someone who actually understands or is at least somewhere near your wavelength. If they are not, then it's not worth feeling bad about what someone says, because they cannot say anything that actually helps or matters. Any time you embody a part of yourself (your thoughts, your creativity, your idea) into an expression, you're opening yourself up to both connection and miscommunication. And that is an impor-

Counterintuitivity · making meaningful innovation

tant distinction; your vision and creativity either land because they are communicated in a language that is understood, or fail to land because they didn't get expressed in a way that moved or connected to someone else's reality. Being creative, visionary, or inspirational is not done solely by a genius.

When we use the term genius, we think of it as a noun, something that represents a person or a group of people, as if it's a way of being. An identity. However, genius is much humbler than that. It's really only a verb. Nobody is a genius all the time, and nobody is a genius in every context. Yet most of us have sprinkles of it that show themselves when we have done the work for it to manifest. People like Einstein embodied it more often than the average person, sure, but even he had limits. In fact, growing up, he was described as average and rather unremarkable. There is a quote often attributed to Albert Einstein (although he likely didn't say it) that says something like: "If you judge a fish by its ability to climb a tree, it will live its whole life believing that it is stupid."

Regardless of whether he said it, it captures an important truth, one that we easily ignore. Genius isn't determined at birth, where if you have it, it's always a part of you, shining through in all that you do. There are some reliable tests in the psychological literature that measure a form of it (IQ), and it does signal the potential for it, but it's not enough. Without the measure of EQ, your genius cannot be communicated or expressed in a manner that does justice to your measure of CQ. How or what mix these three quotients need to activate your genius is the unknown recipe. Design is making intentional choices. Creativity is finding novel connections among familiar ideas. You don't get either unless you are continuously learning and observing the world around you. Each of us has a trigger that unlocks the creativity hidden inside our thoughts and action.

08 Is it only the lucky few?

Creative thinkers and doers are now at the forefront of shaping a new economy and a new future, by being visionary thinkers who follow their path consistently. Visions are the driving force behind meaningful innovations that influence or even change social structure, behaviors and interactions. Turning creativity into innovation growth for a business or brand has a few, seemingly obvious, practices that can be prioritized. However, creativity is very different from other disciplines. People in every discipline learn the limits of the tools and materials they work with. If you are an electrical engineer, you know the conductivity of various metals and a hundred ways to use the voltmeter. If you are a civil engineer, you know the load bearing properties of wood, concrete, and metal. If you a chemical engineer, you know how to optimally know the pH properties of various liquids. You get what I am saying; we work within the possibilities and range of the tools we use. But being creative is different. If you are tapping into your creativity, your basic building material is human intellect and the primary tool is you, and the range you have is determined between your capabilities and limitations.

And therein lies the challenge. In my eyes, people who declare themselves as noncreative or poorly creative are those who struggle, knowingly or not, with expressing a part of their identity. It's why we admire those who fearlessly do so, and why, in turn, this act of creativity seems so out of reach and only for the lucky few. It is not. Creativity is how you see your world. How you make sense of something new or unknown. What stops most of us is the self-criticism and auto-filtering of our own thoughts and questions. We don't want to sound "off" or appear as if we are the only one who doesn't get it. We don't want to risk having to explain ourselves more if our idea or thinking does not land. We avoid that challenge. It's safer to be invisible. How many ideas are lost because they were never expressed or voiced?

Counterintuitivity · making meaningful innovation

"In the wholeheartedness of concentration," the poet, Jane Hirshfield[34], wrote in her beautiful inquiry into the effortless effort of creativity, "world and self begin to cohere. With that state comes an enlarging: of what may be known, what may be felt, what may be done." Such wholehearted concentration is indeed a difficult art, and its difficulty lies in the constant conciliation of the tensions between self and world—a difficulty hardly singular to the particular conditions of our time. Two hundred years before the onslaught of social media, the great French artist, Eugène Delacroix[35], lamented the necessary torment of avoiding social distractions in creative work. A century and a half later, Agnes Martin[36] admonished aspiring artists to exercise discernment in the interruptions they allow, or else corrupt the mental, emotional, and spiritual privacy where inspiration arises. In today's world of notification and constant information loading, self-distraction is the most hazardous kind of distraction, and the most difficult to protect creative thinking against.

Creativity is not something separate from the mind, it simply resides beyond the clutter of everyday thought. An unedited and undiluted manifestation of mind itself. It's something to—well—keep in mind for those times we feel ourselves, or see others, lacking creative thought, struggling with ideas or solving a problem. There are days we feel we just cannot get there. As if it is us that cannot will our way into creative thought. If we step back from that, we start to find a space in our mind, from which our innate creativity arises. And that is the place to rest the mind in. Not staying with distracting thoughts and narratives, but finding a new space where new thoughts and possibilities can be imagined. Without previous ones clouding them, or them getting lost in the everyday chatter. Doing this, each of us will find our mind becoming really interesting in that

---

[34] https://www.poetryfoundation.org/poets/jane-hirshfield
[35] https://www.eugene-delacroix.com/
[36] https://www.artsy.net/article/artsy-editorial-agnes-martin-artist

08 Is it only the lucky few?

thought, that possibility, that we imagine. We will find our mind and being to be relaxed. Two main components to allow imagination to become creative thought. It's why we have our best ideas when we let go of the focus of thinking and give ideas the space and freedom to just happen. It's a potential that each of us can tap into. It's what we should enable more of.

One doesn't manage creativity. One manages for creativity. Your role as a leader in innovation is to create a working environment in which critical thinking, new ideas, and creative solutions can flow unencumbered. I see it as my role to help evoke other people's thoughts and imaginations so that I get a glimpse of the world as they see and understand it. This needs a safe environment because expressing a new creative idea means you differentiate against what is known and accepted. Big and bold ideas challenge our collective imagination, such as paper money, or the individual ownership of a car. When we hear about something that does not fit our universal truths, we often meet it with harsh criticism and deflection. We are caught off guard by the unexpected. Our minds are trained, from early age onward, to think and look for predictability. And yet, being creative by nature, we are anything but predictable.

People's imaginations are like books in the library of the world—seven billion books to explore, too many for one lifetime. There are seven billion creatives on Planet Earth, each with views, assumptions, associations, and seemingly random, often nonsensical thoughts.

How wonderfully unpredictable!

Counterintuitivity · making meaningful innovation

PART 2 • QUESTIONING THE QUESTIONS

chapter 9

Is It Failure Or Incompetence?

IF THERE IS no data, the data has to be created. That does not mean plugging random numbers into your spreadsheet and doing percentage pogo. It means generating real insight from nothing. The more user-centric your effort, the more effort needs to be made to go and meet those users. Study them, understand them. It's not informed by marketing metrics or desktop research. It's done by a mixture of design and anthropological research practices. Those are often seen as a cost, a wasted effort, and of no value to aforementioned numbers. I refer to these "affordable losses" in the interest of learning, creativity, and discovery as "little bets." Because the people we want to innovate for do not live in numbers. They live in the real world.

This seems like common sense; so why is it so hard? Three words: fear of failure. If you're an MBA-trained manager or executive, the odds are you were never, at any point in your educational or professional career, given permission to fail, even on a "little bet." Your parents wanted you to achieve, achieve, achieve—in sports, the

09 Is it failure or incompetence?

classroom, and at work. Your teachers penalized you for having the "wrong" answers, or knocked your grades down if you were imperfect, according to whatever way they defined perfection.

Similarly, modern industrial management is still predicated largely on mitigating risks and preventing errors, not innovating or inventing. Corporate and professional reputation is everything, and the condition of always first needing to know the answers prior to allowing the question to be asked is—for a lot of legacy brands—an unwritten, non-negotiable rule.

Meanwhile, entrepreneurs and designers think of failure the way most people think of learning. We're the ones who feel we must make lots of mistakes to discover new approaches, opportunities, or business models. Like Howard Schultz[37]. When he started Il Giornale in Seattle, the company that Schultz used to later buy the original Starbucks brand and assets, the store had nonstop opera music playing, menus written in Italian, and no chairs; standing bars only. As Schultz has often said, "We had to make a lot of mistakes" before discovering a model that worked.

How is "failure" defined in the pursuit of innovation? If a company you started is going bankrupt, then, yes, that is a failure, and I can empathize. However, if your internalized view of failure is 'anything that is not perfect,' then you are disempowering yourself from exercising your inherent creativity. You're certainly not the only one shackled by the fear of failure, and I don't blame you with the way our educational system is focused so rigidly on "correct answers" and standardized testing. This must change. As must modern management systems; these must become far more adaptive. Leaders need to develop a discovery mindset for those situations where

---

[37] https://www.forbes.com/profile/howard-schultz/

Counterintuitivity · making meaningful innovation

there are many unknowns and uncertainties. Instead of focusing on completing solutions, innovation leaders focus on providing tools and resources to drive a discovery mindset, to identify problems first before jumping in with solutions. And, to do so, they have to change a bunch of internal review approaches so that it becomes cool to be imperfect at the early stages of new projects—so long as you're learning quickly.

One little imperfection after the other, GE, Cisco, Procter & Gamble, and many other companies are on the path to becoming more adaptive. Amazon and Pixar are leaders already. Bill Hewlett[38], co-founder of Hewlett Packard, an ardent proponent of what he called "small bet" innovation, found that HP needed to make 100 small bets to find six breakthroughs[39]. Whether a small bet or an imperfect approach, each are efforts to turn a corporate culture of predictable performance into an innovative culture of proposing possibilities.

Such innovative cultures are generally depicted as pretty fun. Chances are, Google, with their office environments and perks, will come to mind. Corporations that aspire to have them would see a different world compared to theirs. When I ask managers to describe their view and expectation of such innovative behavior, I usually get a list of characteristics identical to those praised enthusiastically by management books: tolerance for failure, willingness to experiment, psychological safety, highly collaborative, and nonhierarchical. Most express confidence in the research that supports that these behaviors translate into better innovative performance. However, despite the fact that this culture is expressed as being desirable, and that most leaders and managers always claim to understand what it

---

[38] https://en.wikipedia.org/wiki/Bill_Hewlett
[39] from https://www.amazon.com/Little-Bets-Breakthrough-Emerge-Discoveries-ebook/dp/B0043RSJTU

09 Is it failure or incompetence?

entails, this culture is hard to create and sustain. In fact, more common is the outright resistance to truly activating it. This is puzzling. How can practices apparently so wanted and understood turn out to be so tricky to implement and adhere to?

I believe the reason is that regardless of the books, seminars, workshops, and trainings, a truly innovative culture is misunderstood. The easy-to-like behaviors that get so much attention are only one side of the coin. The counterbalance involves some tougher and frankly less than fun behaviors.

You see, a tolerance for failure requires an intolerance for incompetence. A willingness to experiment requires rigorous discipline. Psychological safety requires comfort with candour and being vulnerable. Collaboration must be balanced with individual accountability. And flatness requires strong leadership. Yes, even innovative cultures are paradoxical, just as their processes are. Unless the tensions created by this paradox are carefully managed, attempts to create an innovative culture where we dare to fail will . . . well; fail.

It is the fear of management's negative reaction to failures that keeps people from bringing up new ideas or pointing out potential problems that could benefit from innovation. Fear will also keep people from admitting to failures that may cost the organization, or withhold a radical innovation that can mean developing a significant new market. It is this fear of failure that management must fight throughout the entire organization. Management's reaction to failure determines whether fear will be a major inhibitor of innovation; this fear can be present at all levels of the organization. Management itself may be afraid to accept and implement innovations for fear that they will fail. When management does not accept failures as part of the innovation process, the fear of failure will cause the organization to focus on incremental innovations that are safer and have less risk. The more meaningful innovations that can change the industry or bring new value to our lives will be avoided because of fear.

A large part of our effort is to help management understand that not all innovations will succeed, not all implemented concepts will be profitable and thus there is an inherent risk. Even when everything is done in a reasoned business process, with data to back up insights, there will still be failures as a normal and acceptable part of innovation development. Without that acceptance, the fear of failure will inhibit the creation of innovative ideas and the attempts to make risk-laden innovative ideas a reality.

One example for handling the failure problem comes from a presentation by John Cleese[40] where he describes **the value of accepting mistakes**. The essence of the concept is that a guided missile must repeatedly receive input on its performance and make adjustments to its trajectory to be able to hit the target. In the business context, if no one admits to mistakes, there will be no corrections and the objective will be missed. If the mistake is only found out at the end, there will typically not be enough time to fix the problem. Thus, admitting to a small mistake, with management and leadership accepting these mistakes as a normal part of determining the best course for the business, is a far superior habit. If, however, people are afraid to admit failures—even the smaller ones—there won't be any corrections until the problem is much worse. Admitting failure is a sign of a healthy organization, one that is optimally conducive to innovation.

---

[40] https://www.videoarts.com/news/the-merits-of-virtual-mistakes/

09 Is it failure or incompetence?

Another such sign is the ability to **accept risks when exploring new ideas** and trying to develop them into marketable concepts. Experimentation will often be essential to innovation, but this, too, may result in a failure. The optimum situation is for management to have a well-defined innovation development process that includes failures as an accepted part of business. In our projects, we spend time exploring what success looks like for the brand we are partnering with. We also explore what failure would look like because it helps shape the realistic expectations for the team and the company to synchronize to. I made a deliberate choice in saying "synchronize" versus "align." If a vision is driving the innovation, there may not be enough evidence or known markers for management to impose their expectations.

There are interesting examples of products that failed to meet their management's expectations for their current marketplace, but then quickly improved to the point where they became the dominant technology. The personal computers developed by Apple and IBM were not products for their existing customers that needed serious computing power. In fact, major electronics and computer companies did not want to produce the first personal computers because they did not see a market for such a product. Apple and IBM managements were willing to take the risk to develop a new product and a new market.

Innovations can be wasteful with experimentation and failures, but they also allow an organization to glean information about why it failed, and from that knowledge develop an innovative perspective that can actually change the marketplace. Failure analysis is the key to finding success through innovation. Some of the most highly touted innovators have had their share of failures. Remember Apple's Newton or MobileMe, Google Glass, and the Amazon Fire Phone?

Some of these were a failure of tactics. Each are 'how' mistakes: a failure to execute on a good strategy and a clear vision. But you can have 'what' mistakes that result in a failure of strategy. When you follow a strategy that fails to deliver the results you want. And there is failure of vision, or when the mistake is the 'why.' When there is no clear direction, or no shared understanding of why you do the things you do.

Despite the ask and the desired culture to tolerate failure, innovative organizations have to be intolerant of incompetence. Innovation asks high-performance standards for those involved. Exploring risky ideas that ultimately fail is fine, but mediocre technical skills, sloppy thinking, bad work habits, and poor management are not. It's the cold shower of this industry. People who don't meet expectations are either let go or moved into roles that better fit their abilities. Steve Jobs was notorious for firing anyone he deemed not up to the task—something he had singular rule over, which I do not recommend as a practice. Building a culture of competence requires clearly articulating expected standards of performance. If such standards are not well understood, they are meaningless and set the effort up for failure. Shifting technologies or business models can render a person who's very competent in one context incompetent in another. Consider how digitization has impacted the value of different skills in many industries.

Keeping people who have been rendered obsolete and show no learning agility may be compassionate, but it's dangerous for the innovation capacities of any organization. Maintaining a healthy balance between tolerating productive failures and rooting out incompetence is not easy. A 2015 New York Times article[41] about Amazon illustrates the difficulty. The piece, which was based on interviews

---

[41] https://www.nytimes.com/2015/08/16/technology/inside-amazon-wrestling-big-ideas-in-a-bruising-workplace.html

09 Is it failure or incompetence?

with more than 100 current and former employees, labeled Amazon's culture as "bruising" and recounted stories of employees crying at their desks amid enormous performance pressures. What collateral do we pay for innovation?

The truth is that a tolerance for failure requires having extremely competent people. Attempts to create novel technological or new business models are ranked with uncertainty, where often you don't know what you don't know, and you have to learn as you go. "Failures" under these circumstances provide valuable lessons about paths forward. Here's where learning agility comes into play. Creating a culture that simultaneously values learning through failure and outstanding performance is difficult in organizations with a history of neither. Revealing the distinct difference between productive and unproductive failures is something innovation leaders need to help communicate often and early.

Simply put; **"Fail fast, fail often" is just bad advice.** That cliché "celebrating failure" misses the entire point—we should be celebrating learning, not failure. A simple prototype that fails to perform as expected because of a previously unknown technical issue is a failure worth celebrating if that new knowledge can be applied to future designs. Failure analysis needs to focus on the learning. If there isn't any value, the reason for failure might, unfortunately, be incompetence.

Counterintuitivity · making meaningful innovation

PART 2 • QUESTIONING THE QUESTIONS

chapter 10
Do We Have To Collaborate?

I'M SURE YOU'VE noticed it; collaboration is the bee's knees. Sliced bread, the new black. It is taking over the workplace, and even found a place on resumes as a skill for some, or a character trait of note for others. As digital innovation becomes increasingly global and cross-functional, silos have to be broken down, and interaction between departments is increasing. Teamwork is touted as the key to organizational and innovational success. Everything and anything is now done "collaboratively." Collaboration creates once-elusive "buy-in" or "empowerment," improves problem solving, increases creativity, and is hailed as the key to innovation. It slashes costs and improves productivity. What's not to like?

Certainly, I find much to applaud in this development. However, when a shift of culture spikes that dramatically, it gives me reasons to pause. I am an employee myself, a valuable resource that in turn needs to provide a return for the company; their profit. As part of that arrangement, the company then honors their commitment of providing me a monetary benefit for it; my salary. That is an indi-

10 Do we have to collaborate?

vidual merit only. Could this already be an indicator of why true collaboration is as rare as it is?

Consider a typical week in your own organization. How much time do you spend in meetings, on the phone, and responding to emails? At many companies, agencies, and consultancies, I would dare state that the proportion hovers around 80%, leaving employees little time for all the critical work they must complete on their own. Performance suffers as they are buried under an avalanche of requests for input or advice, access to resources, decisions to make, votes to be voiced, follow-ups across multiple different software platforms, and being present at a meeting. Sure, we will feel in demand, but we will feel disengaged. It's not possible to hold that bandwidth and energy to perform at our best, deliver the value we have, or want to give and feel ownership.

What's more, it is my observation—for what it is worth—that the distribution of collaborative work is often rather lopsided. In most cases, the real value-adding collaborations come from only a few team members. As those people become known for being both capable and willing to help, they are drawn into projects and roles of growing importance. Their giving mindset and desire to help others quickly enhances their performance and reputation. But this only further fuels the demands placed on top collaborators and puts in question the actual benefit of what we call "collaboration." That what starts as a virtuous cycle, the "let's collaborate" soon turns vicious. Soon capable collaborators become innovation bottlenecks: nothing progresses until they've weighed in. Worse, they are so overtaxed that they're no longer personally effective. And more often than not, the volume and diversity of work they do to benefit others goes unnoticed, because the requests are coming from other units or even multiple companies. In our quest to innovate, we want

Counterintuitivity · making meaningful innovation

to reap the rewards of collaboration but have inadvertently done so without recognizing the holistic costs. What can innovation leaders do to manage these demands more effectively, and optimize true collaboration?

Collaboration can be difficult. As a word alone, collaboration seems abstract, conjuring up images of people always being together. On top of this, collaboration involves the complexities of human beings. Encouraging people to work together toward a shared mission may not be successful if you don't convey or provide an incentive. What is often not considered is that, at the core, collaboration is a choice. Anyone involved first has to make the conscious choice to do this. I dismiss the premise that collaboration is fixed because there is a wide spectrum of what teamwork and partnerships can look like, so you can begin to learn and experience the benefits of collaboration. First, however, we can't manage collaboration well until we acknowledge that it's fundamentally dangerous. Collaboration is walking on eggshells. Every time and all the time.

How so? Just consider how vulnerable people feel when they do not know the answers, but are in a group that is put together in order to find them. The fundamental premise of collaboration is that you can use it to solve complex problems that are beyond the function of one domain or expertise. That means that each participant needs to be comfortable with a certain amount of ambiguity. Most people have built their careers—perhaps even their identity—on being the expert. In the spectrum of collaboration, there is friction between roles and functions. Requiring a social architecture that clarifies the roles and makes it visible when there is discomfort. Role and responsibilities in the collaboration space tend not to be hierarchical; they are often fluid, changing from phase to phase of the work. This can be especially hard for senior executives because it may mean be-

10 Do we have to collaborate?

coming part of the "tribe of doing things." For others, the opposite is their new reality; within a team, they hold more presence or have a stronger voice than outside of it. Collaboration comes with the illusion of democracy. But that is often not the premise to deliver the best work.

Collaboration means a shift from thinking big ideas alone and moving into the real-time mess of thinking with others. Again, a big ask when you have built a career, or see others be successful in the application of the "I tell, they do" model. Changing the behavior to a "we think together" model is the central activity of a collaboration. Because thinking together closes a gap; people can now act without checking back in because they were there when the decision was made. They've already had the debates about all the trade-offs that actually make something work. This may appear a case of "when all was said and done, a lot more was said than done." However, time needs to be spent in the messy and time-consuming front-loaded process of thinking through possibilities, in order to inform the decision that needs to be made. Too much talking and not enough doing is a feeling that only happens when decisions are not informed or shared. For collaboration to work, information is rarely left in a silo but is shared and often combined in unexpected ways to reframe problems. This is the part of the process most creatives revel and look forward to. But for some people, especially those new to that kind of thinking, this can mean information overload and analysis paralysis. For others, who withhold information in order to retain power, this need for a free flow of information and an openness to discuss or question it, is threatening. Collaborating means dealing with conflicting priorities; more eggshells. Boundaries aren't always clear. If you want to avoid conflict, or don't know how to disagree effectively, nothing will happen. Knowing how to debate the trade-offs between many viable options means knowing

Counterintuitivity · making meaningful innovation

how to argue with each other in more open and visible ways. Not doing this well, or doing that wrong—or simply avoiding that? Very risky. Very dangerous.

As mentioned earlier, often, collaboration happens on top of other work. Most of us are already plenty busy with our "day job" and the new projects in which we are asked to go in and contribute may be especially stressful because of this. Until the problems that any collaboration project is aimed to fix gets solved, such projects can often be overwhelming, even for those who do it day to day. The notion still persists; if we would just collaborate, then we would do better! But as already described, collaboration is about the friction of ideas and the forging of new ways of working. That is not easy, or even nice. It makes new demands on all of us. It means leaders must do more than just tell people what to do. It also means people within the C-suite of an organization have to avoid seagull tactics, and do more than fly in, make noise, point at what's broken, and then delicately walk away. If collaboration is aimed to hear all opinions, then we must actively listen to all of them. But again, the danger here is the sense of democratic exchanges and equal value to all contributions. It shouldn't be. Collaborating is not done so some of us can hide, and others can feel good about their knowledge or power or role. People need to be heard, but also need to hear, all the contributions in thinking and creating, so that they understand why the business picks one priority over another. Leaders in this effort need to make those calls and direct the focus. While keeping the momentum and egos unscratched. Tricky thing to pull off—collaborative projects are judged on the outcome, more than the individual efforts that went into them. The importance of understanding and decoding resistance cannot be ignored. And because this will friction between being authoritative and influential, these efforts are more secondary layers of work for leaders. More dirt under fingernails.

10 Do we have to collaborate?

When everyone has a voice and uses it, there is an increased importance of social validation within these groups, so it is clear who to praise and who to blame.

Inherently, collaboration says something is happening outside of one's immediate control. Collaborative work is not right for every organization, or in every innovation initiative. It works best for organizations that need to solve problems across different parts of the business, where cross-pollination of ideas improves the output, where speed to market is crucial, and when getting people to co-own the solution will create more velocity in the execution of the work. Those working cultures are not all that prevalent. That said, walk around any organization and ask the question, "are you a good collaborator?" I would bet that regardless of who you ask, they all say "yes." This is one of the biggest collaboration problems. And no one wants to talk about it. Collaboration doesn't have a unifying methodology—it is situational. It's not a technique or skill as much as it is a behavior and attitude. Most people make poor collaborative choices every day without knowing it and believe they are still good at collaborating. If that were true, why do we have a plethora of collaborative software solutions flooding the industry today?

Using collaborative tools won't solve this problem. There are hundreds of software solutions flooding the workspace today. You've probably used some variation of collaboration tools at some office gig you've had. Some of the big names are Slack, Trello, Basecamp, and Asana—but honestly, Microsoft Online and Google Drive are basically collaboration tools as well. It's pretty much anything that can allow a team to work across a series of projects and deliverables.

For me, collaborative tools are missing the point. They have gotten a bunch of attention from the business media and some corporate leaders in the past few years—there was even a feeling by many that Slack could revolutionize the entire idea of the workplace. Yet, none of these tools solves the actual problem; **what if people honestly don't want to collaborate?** Successful collaboration is a behavioral issue, and one that most vendors of collaborative software solutions want nothing to do with. They offer a digital version to replace and centralize a physical action. What if people don't actually enjoy collaboration at work? Like any what-if question, it can be asked with a grain of salt—but I've seen this in a lot of places I've worked, too. People want to be rewarded and know they're doing well. Companies promote individuals even though they work in teams. This is a practical issue in collaboration, including collaboration tools: ten people need to come together to hit a deliverable and advance the company in some way, right? But then only one of those 10 will get a bump in performance, only one is seen as responsible for the outcomes. If you're consistently in that 90%-bucket, you'll eventually get tired of what you're doing. It happens to most people.

The second problem these tools are not mitigating is any concept of cross-functional collaboration in companies. Silos are a really powerful thing. We train people to think about work as a series of functional expertise moments. Silos. Innovation culture now is business-need-driven and/or customer-need-driven. It's not driven by "I'm the marketing guy" or "I meet sales targets," yet most companies are still set up that way. Again, it goes back to basic human psychology—if you work in IT, you have a chain of command and set bosses. Those bosses should be the ones theoretically driving your workflow. Operating out of their narrow world view; their belief the world is either flat or at the center of everything. But then marketing needs to work with IT on some emarketing solution, and suddenly you're beholden to a bunch of new people with new vocabulary and new methodologies.

10 Do we have to collaborate?

Collaboration isn't easy for many people even though it has become a gold staple of corporate buzzwords for executives trying to prove how functional and innovative their organization is. Because people love processes. Most processes in a company are simply 'process for the sake of process'—they don't really move anything forward, they just make some middle manager feel more comfortable with a spreadsheet he/she has to maintain. It is a wonder that the tools we create to enhance collaboration really are but glorified document file cabinets?

I don't know about you, but I am still waiting for digital collaboration tools that can actually help make teams better. At my current company, we use our share of internally allocated and appointed collaboration software platforms and social constructs as well. Collaboration, for an experience design company, is crucial. And, even though we can genuinely say we enjoy spending time with each other, we would be lying if we said productive collaboration always came naturally. Like any business, we run also into communication issues. We question whether we have the right people in the right roles on the right projects. Some of us work best in short bursts, others need longer spans of time to be productive. Some love structure, others need room to breathe and create. In short, we're all different (which is great)—but sometimes, our different preferences, approaches, and paces can make collaboration more difficult. It's just natural.

As a highly collaborative practitioner in a highly collaborative business, I would be wrong to push aside these challenges. In the same way that I can transform a business through empathy, I can transform a team through empathy. Much of the value of this assessment is the respect that comes with acknowledging that we don't all approach or process things in the same way. Understanding that people come at work from different angles and accommodating or flexing to what people need to be successful can mean a lot. It can fuel more productive collaboration and better decision making. If you surprise someone who needs time to look at the details with an impromptu meeting, understand that this isn't optimal for their way of processing information. Try to give them a bit of warning next time, or explain the urgency of this particular situation. Similarly, before you jump into the details with anyone who processes through emotion, try to take a step back and just ask them how their days are going. It's little things like this that can help build a better functioning team. Again; none of which is accommodated or instructed by any of the hailed collaborative tools we are asked to use.

It's not an issue of ease of use. Nor of iterating them to better features. All collaboration software is designed to be intuitive and frictionless in how they are used. It's actually an issue of being too easy to use, all the time, any time. Personal responsibility and poor self-control are always a factor, but users need to be aware that most digital tools are engineered to elicit compulsive behavior. They're designed to make you feel productive without actually being productive. I can't fault Slack or any of the other tools for being well-designed and easy to use—their designers did their job well. It's our job to make sure we use it, and other tools like it, responsibly and with a clear understanding that collaboration is a choice of a behavior much more than it is a choice of tools or processes. The atomic unit of collaboration is an interaction between two people. But knowing how to interact and what to do in each situation requires judgment, awareness, and practical skills which need to be taught and experienced. We can teach skills, but judgment and awareness in a collaborative situation come from experience.

10 Do we have to collaborate?

I define working/thinking/doing together as a series of interactions between two or more people for a specific purpose or goal. There is a scale (fig.6) I use to differentiate "collaboration" from many of the other terms used for it. Each of these begins with an assumption of differences. Different people with different capabilities in different business units, working for different outcomes. There are four C's that are each 'the same but different':

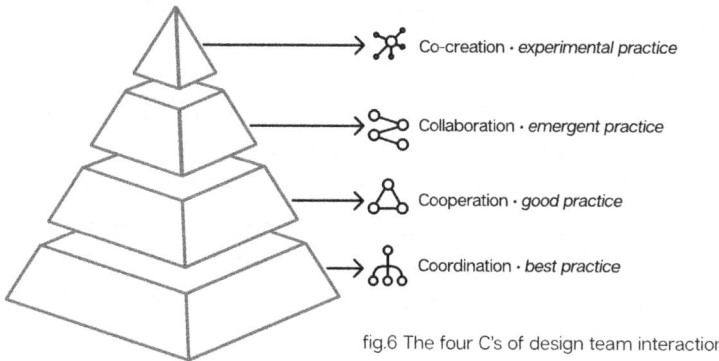

fig.6 The four C's of design team interaction

Coordination applies the 'best practice' situations where the challenge is familiar, the process is clear, the solution is known, the delivery of success straight forward. It's all about effectiveness—for example, production line work, the kitchen in a restaurant, the construction of a house. All are clear on their specific roles and when/how to do what they uniquely do—together—understanding the relationships between them, their individual contributions, and what the coordinated whole achieves.

Cooperation is a step up and is also about differences. However, these differences now come together not to merely roll out a solution as effectively as possible, instead, they are bringing their subject matter expertise to bear on a particular challenge, where there may be several potential—definable—solutions at play. Cooperation means being able to work effectively across the perceived team or organizational boundary lines, working within agreed ground rules, sharing information, challenging constructively, and using appropriate decision-making protocols. Cooperation applies in more complicated situations where 'good practice' will be the best approach given there may be several ways to resolve a tricky challenge.

Collaboration is not about agreement and playing by the rules. It's the friction caused by competition of ideas, the ambiguity of uncertainty around solving the problem, and the originality of the creativity in play. That creativity often comes from the sparks of disagreement, dissent, and even conflict as collaboration seeks divergent insights and spontaneity, not structural or cultural harmony. It's more emergent in nature, rather than pursuing best or good practice approaches, therefore, participants must be prepared for higher failure rates than would be tolerated generally in the organization.

And lastly, the pinnacle of these interactions, is **Co-Creation**. Which is always anchored with purpose and vision—the pursuit of a specific result or the solving of a wicked problem in order to create new value. Undefined problems with a series of polarities, seemingly unrealistic outcomes are envisioned. Co-creation applies in more complex situations which require an 'experimental practice' approach in order to solve adaptive challenges in the face of disruption or the development of a behavioral changing systemic solution. Whenever a group of people can explore a new approach to tackle or explore sudden new-problem or opportunity spaces, you will find a potential need for co-creation. Where the way the team responds is co-determined, along with what or why it is they are responding that way. Co-creation teamwork is the highest form in that it also requires the highest competencies of those involved. There are clear

10 Do we have to collaborate?

accountable contributions to the decisions, but these are based on a shared understanding and a joined effort in shaping choices first.

It is no surprise that—by and large—the innovation efforts that are demanding collaboration are, in fact, delivered by cooperation. It's human nature; along with our instinct for self-preservation, that we also have an instinct to belong, to get along with each other, so that the sum of our efforts produce an outcome that is greater than what we would have been able to produce by acting in our own self-interest. Evolution has directly tied our ability to survive to our ability to cooperate.

Well-functioning innovation systems need information, input, and significant integration of effort from a diverse array of contributors. People who work in a collaborative culture view seeking help from colleagues as natural, regardless of whether providing such help is within their colleagues' formal job descriptions. They have a sense of collective responsibility. But too often, collaboration gets confused with consensus. And consensus is poison for rapid decision making and navigating the complex problems associated with transformational innovation. Ultimately, someone has to make a decision and be accountable for it. An accountability culture is one where individuals are expected to make decisions and own the consequences. Accountability and collaboration can be complementary, and accountability can drive collaboration. Consider an organization where you will be personally held accountable for specific decisions. There is no hiding. You own the decisions you make, for better or worse. The last thing you would do is shut yourself off from feedback or from enlisting the cooperation and collaboration of people inside and outside the organization who can help you. Leaders can encourage accountability by publicly holding themselves accountable, even when that creates personal risks.

Counterintuitivity · making meaningful innovation

I say it again: we can't manage collaboration well until we acknowledge that it's fundamentally a dangerous thing to do. Aside from learning to share toys in kindergarten, formal education gives very few lessons on how to collaborate. This explains why in the majority of projects, there is not much collaboration in play. Certainly not as much as we are assuming there is. Yet this is a time when teamwork is becoming the norm and teams are more often than not made up of contractors or consultants from outside the organization. Collaborative skill improvement can be a unique and effective way to dramatically increase team performance. In my experience, unhealthy collaboration scenarios most often stem from two underlying maladies: organizational complexity and a "collaboration for collaboration's sake" culture. Take meetings, for instance. If meetings become the norm for how work gets done in an organization, an individual employee can do very little. Over time, meetings become a status symbol—that is, the more meetings to which an executive is invited, the more important he or she is assumed to be. Even worse, meetings can become a substitute for effective leadership communication. Rather than taking the time to share the specifics discussed in a meeting with those who did not attend, some leaders opt to invite just about everyone to every meeting. As bosses fail to cascade vital information to their staff following important meetings, employees come to believe that they need to attend every meeting or risk missing out. So, what starts out as a well-intentioned drive for inclusiveness turns into a downward spiral of more meetings and wasted time.

But it doesn't have to be this way. There is much to like—and dread—about collaboration in the workplace. We have all grown weary of the needless meetings, unnecessary emails, and other unproductive interactions associated with collaboration at work. Excessive collaboration saps energy and leaves employees with too

10 Do we have to collaborate?

little time to complete their work during the day. Leaders must learn to recognize, promote, and efficiently distribute the right kinds of collaborative work, or their teams and top talent will bear the costs of too much demand for too little supply. Collaboration is a "hands-on" activity of nurturing a culture where ideas may come from anywhere. If we do not truly understand the distinctions between the different ways people can work together in the pursuit of the innovation, and that this can swing between coordination, cooperation, co-creation as well as collaboration, we risk developing innovative ideas in ways that are meaningless to those involved. This can swing between coordinating, cooperating, co-creating as well as collaborating.

If we do not truly understand the distinctions between the different ways people can work together in the pursuit of innovations, we risk developing innovative ideas in ways that are meaningless to those involved.

Part 3
Acting on what matters

"status quo, you know,
is Latin for
the mess we're in."

—Ronald Reagan, Actor,
40th president of the United States

Counterintuitivity · making meaningful innovation

PART 3 • ACTING ON WHAT MATTERS

chapter 11
Stop Digging Deeper Holes

GROWING UP, I deeply admired my grandfather's abilities. He was of a generation that made what they needed. He extended the house my mother grew up in, crafted the doors in it. Fixed what was broken, and enhanced what could work better. He was also one heck of a fisher. On weekend visits, I would see him and one of my uncles walk back into the kitchen—via the back porch he constructed—with the fishing rods in one hand and a bunch of fish in the other. In my eight-year-old schoolboy mind, he held the secrets to everything. I must have overwhelmed him with my questions because he often answered them somewhat cryptically, I spent hours trying to figure out what was so secretive about it. For example, I vividly remember the moment I asked him, "Why are you such a good fisher?" To which he simply replied, "Because I know where the fish are biting."

Intended or not, Grandpa (*Pepe*, as my sisters and I called him) offered life advice: know where the fish are biting and fish there. Our consumer and manufacturing industries are looking to do just that; react to customer demand. Industry specialists have a framework for that purpose; it is known as a **pull strategy**. Analysts categorize and segment consumer populations and build innovations to satisfy their desires. Then, designers build new products when we know there is a demand. Pull strategies give people what they think they want. That is; only what they want now, not what they'll want next. Pull strategies result in product bloat and feature creep: you make too many things that you can't sustain and end up with legacy products that don't do much of anything for anyone.

This is known and understood by those same industry specialists, so there is another framework on hand to avoid the downsides of a pull strategy. It is the opposite motion, known as a **push strategy**. Driven by new technologies, a manufacturer will make a product that holds that novelty and then market it as the amenity that everyone supposedly wants and needs.

Simply put, a push strategy is to push a product at a customer, while a pull strategy pulls a customer toward a product. Push strategy is a quick way to move a customer from awareness to purchase, while pull strategy is about creating an ongoing relationship with the brand. Both serve a purpose in moving the customer along the journey from awareness to purchase. So companies balance both, with the theory that it should be done carefully and with a thorough understanding of your business, current brand awareness, and target audience. For example, launching a new, unknown product would require more push than an established brand.

The thing is, both push and pull strategies will get a company stuck in the hole of a planning cycle. Because the reality is that customer preferences or attitudes are not consistent, predictable, or stable. These, like every aspect of innovations, are prone to change

Counterintuitivity · making meaningful innovation

over time. Pull strategies do not account for any shift in system or demographics, missing out on accommodating any new kinds of behavior or desires. When that happens, you are up for a disruption.

For example, companies like Uber and Airbnb saw an unfilled need in the overlooked, burgeoning sector of millennials who, unlike their boomer elders, don't aspire to own cars and don't want to live in big houses. They have currently embraced the on-demand lifestyle. All the major car-rental companies and hoteliers—with their pull strategies—completely missed out on this tremendous shift in behavior. It isn't just an anomaly: it is a pattern. Kodak[42] should have been in prime position to own the digital photo market, Sony[43] owned portable music, etc. The list can be extended with various other missed opportunities by brands who had the means and the ability to understand the shortcomings of their tactics. Instead, they kept their old antiquated habits.

That habit is to plan. Using only what they assume to know, and the signals they see as the future. The thing is that the future they see is only giving them a present. Rather than the present being able to give them a future. And while they are planning, the world is advancing and the opportunities you are planning for are disappearing. Neither of these approaches is sophisticated enough to keep up with the increasing speed and magnitude that innovation needs to happen in order to be meaningful for our society.

It's rule number one in the **Law of Holes: if you are stuck in one, stop digging.** There are alternative strategies developing in forward-thinking circles, that can supplement these somewhat obsolete push/pull strategies. One such is scenario-planning; a creative strategy that looks at the elements possibly driving the future and

---
[42] https://www.forbes.com/sites/chunkamui/2012/01/18/how-kodak-failed/
[43] https://www.ft.com/content/7558a99e-f5ed-11e1-a6c2-00144feabdc0

11 Stop digging deeper holes

then considers all the alternatives and variations to these elements by making stories out of them. In telling these stories, we can start to figure out what these unknown situations might actually look or feel like. And more importantly, what it would all mean for those involved.

There is discovery-driven planning that goes even further than scenario-planning. It comes from the work[44] of Columbia Professor Rita McGrath[45], who tells us that when things aren't going exactly as planned, key indicators need to be identified, and then investigated to try to figure out which ones aren't performing well and determine the causes of those failures. Then, a contingency is planned with some fine-tuning in real time so that these events can be avoided or capitalized on, depending on whether they're a challenge or an opportunity. Other models are offering alternative approaches to solve the shortcomings of a push-and-pull strategy. But ultimately, it drills down to a cold, hard fact of life: our future cannot be predicted.

Those active in innovation, or the entrepreneurship around it, are equated with the term futurists. As if the new idea or vision that they declare was formed out of a knowledge of what the future needs. Anticipating outcomes is a human trait that has gotten us where we are today. This capacity has become a wavering calculus to derive the world, and evaluate its immensely large, complex systems and structures, with the aim to know where we can tune or modify, and pre-determine our behaviors and attitudes toward it. Somehow, it has us believing that, as humans, we have dominion over the future.

Yet we routinely fail to predict the important stuff, even with the use of sophisticated algorithms that chew through impossibly large

---
[44] https://www.strategy-business.com/article/00239?gko=ede47
[45] https://www.ritamcgrath.com/

Counterintuitivity · making meaningful innovation

volumes of data to offer dozens upon dozens of pattern-based simulations. It says less about the methodologies of foresight and more about our tragic aspiration to know the unknown. The future simply cannot be predicted. If a future is known, it is by default no longer a future. If we claim to know just how a change will occur, it is no longer a change. As they say, change is the only constant. Models do some leg work and help limit the unwanted outcomes that could happen. But the real world is rife with non-linearity, countering the logic of a data pattern. Like stock market crashes, riots, and earthquakes, discontinuities warp linear projections with sudden disruptions that often defy prediction.

For millennia, we've grappled with unpredictability pretty well. All things considered, we are the dominant species because of our innate talent to adapt and survive. But our societies are vastly different now. Here's a creative experiment for you; take a typical man, an average Joe of sorts, on a given street in the year 1900 and then drop him, Back to the Future-style, into the 1950s. Then take someone from the 1950s and move him into the present day. Who would experience the greater change?

The answer will seem fairly obvious; if a person from the turn of the 20th century was to be time-warped into the 1950s, they'd be baffled and in awe of the numerous technological wonders. He would see streets and highways jammed with sleek cars, trucks, and buses. In the cities, immense skyscrapers would line the horizon, and inside, elevators would whisk him up. Gigantic bridges would span rivers where once only ferries could cross. There would be flying machines overhead, carrying people across continents and oceans in a matter of hours rather than days or weeks. Visiting a home, this time-traveler would enter a strange new environment filled with appliances powered by electricity: sounds and moving

11 Stop digging deeper holes

images on a device called television, musical programs and news bulletins from a box known as radio. He would see refrigerators to keep things cold, washing machines to clean his clothes, and a contraption that makes him able to dial up other people and have a conversation with them, even if they lived in another town, state, or country; a telephone.

The house's garden would be an area of relaxation, with perhaps a flower bed, and almost certainly a lawn. But no more need for a vegetable patch because this concept called "supermarket" offers an array of technologically enhanced foods, year round. Things like instant coffee and frozen vegetables. Life itself would be dramatically extended. Many once-fatal ailments are now prevented with an injection or cured with a pill. The newness of this time-traveler's physical surroundings should be profoundly disorienting for him.

I would, however, imagine that someone from the 1950s would have little trouble navigating the physical landscape of today. Ours is the age of boundless technological wonders, but I think that our second time-traveler would find himself in a world not all that different from the one he came from.

He would still drive a car to work, although he could opt to have himself driven. If he took the train, it would likely be on the same line leaving from the same station as it did back in the 1950s. He could probably board a more modern airplane at the same airport, too. He would still live in a suburban house, though a bigger one. His television would have more channels, color pictures, and bigger, flatter screens. He could still catch some of his favorite 1950s shows on reruns. With just a few exceptions, such as the Internet, CD and DVD players, the cash machine, and wireless phones and entertainment systems that slip into his pocket, he would be familiar with almost all current-day technology. I would, in fact, not be surprised if our time-traveller is rather disappointed by the pace of progress. "Why haven't we conquered outer space?" "Where are all the robots?" "Why can't my car fly?" It's fair to say that, on the basis of big, obvious technological changes alone, the 1900-to-1950s traveler would experience the greater shift, whereas the other might easily conclude that we'd spent the second half of the twentieth century doing little more than iterating on the great innovations that had so transformed its first half.

However, the longer they stayed in their new homes, the more each time-traveler would become aware of the subtler dimensions of change. Each would begin to notice their respective society's changed norms and values. They would notice the different ways in which everyday people live and work. And when taking in account the effort of adjusting to the social structures and the rhythms and patterns of daily life, it would be our second time-traveler who would likely be much more disoriented.

Because someone living the early 1900s would find the social world of the 1950s remarkably similar to his own. If our traveler worked in a factory, he would come to find much of the same divisions of labor, the same hierarchical systems of control. If he worked in an office setting, he'd work within the same bureaucracy, and have the same climb up the corporate ladder. He would deliver a 9–5 working day wearing a suit and tie, and his colleagues and management would mostly be white and male. If there were women in his workplace, they would be secretaries. He would almost never interact professionally with someone of another race. He would marry young, have children quickly thereafter, stay married to the same person, and probably work for the same company for the rest of his life. In his leisure time, his recreational activities would be much

11 Stop digging deeper holes

the same as they were in 1900: taking in a baseball game or a boxing match, maybe playing a round of golf. He would join the clubs and civic groups befitting his socioeconomic class, observe the same social distinctions, and fully expect his children to do likewise. He would find himself living the life of the "company man."

In contrast, our second time-traveller is going to be rattled by the dizzying social and cultural changes that have happened between his 1950s and today. At work, he would find a new dress code, a new schedule, and new rules. He would see office workers dressed like folks relaxing on the weekend in jeans and open-necked shirts and be shocked to learn that some of them occupy positions of authority. People at the office would seemingly come and go as they pleased. Quite a few have these incomprehensible piercings and tattoos. Women and even non-whites would be managers, leaders, or clients. Individuality and self-expression would be valued over conformity. His working environment would be packed with people who seem principled, and political correctness is a new variable for him. He cannot even smoke unless in the parking lot. Attitudes and expressions he had never thought about would cause repeated offence. He would continually suffer the painful feeling of not knowing how to behave.

This time-traveler would see different ethnic groups in greater numbers than he could ever have imagined—Asian, Indian, Afro and Latin Americans, and others—mingling in ways he likely would find inappropriate. Especially the mixed-race couples and same-sex couples. People would seem to be always working and yet never working when they were supposed to. They would strike him as lazy and yet obsessed with exercise. They would seem career-conscious yet fickle—why doesn't anybody stay with a company more than three years? What happened to the ladies' clubs, Moose Lodges, and bowling leagues? Why doesn't everybody go to church? Even though the physical surroundings would be relatively familiar, the feel of the place would be bewilderingly different.

Although the first time-traveller had to adjust to some drastic technological changes, it is the second who experiences the deeper, more pervasive transformation. It is the second who has been thrust into a time when lifestyles and worldviews are most assuredly changing—a time when the old order has broken down, when flux and uncertainty themselves seem to be part of the everyday norm. Where the predictions of the future were giving us flying cars and robots, what seemed to have been less understood or anticipated is the change of the fabric of society and the different ecosystems that would emerge.

Systems are complex interactions of interdependent parts that give rise to emergent and often-unexpected behaviors. If you, like me, have ever kept an aquarium, you have a sense for the delicate equilibrium necessary to a healthy aquatic system. Add a new fish or trim too much of the plants, and you can suddenly veer into an ecosystem crash. Small changes can have large results, so you have to be very deliberate in how you manage the tank. Meaningful analysis requires careful scoping: what to include and what to dismiss. Typically, we think in terms of linear cause and effect. Add too much salt to your aquarium and things start to die. Not enough, and you have the same result. You could plot this relationship as a straight line: salt concentration vs. number of living fish. But that is only of relevance in a closed system. One with defined boundaries and conditions. That is not our world today. We have open systems that interplay. Much like how one ecosystem, a coral reef, interacts with another system; a saltwater ocean. In a saltwater reef, many actors participate in the ecosystem. Corals build reefs that harbor diverse

11 Stop digging deeper holes

species. Snails and crabs clean detritus. Sea plants filter the water and lower nitrogen. Fish eat algae and organisms, excreting waste that raises nitrogen levels. In this type of living system, changes can quickly propagate across interdependent actors toward a sudden tipping point. Not enough fish can allow algae to bloom and kill off the corals that support reef health, leading to an ecosystem crash. But so can nutrient flows from farming along rivers that dump into coastal waters, or changes to water temperature from regional warming trends. In complex, inter-dependent ecosystems, changes can happen suddenly when equilibrium is pushed to its edges. Such systems are considered non-linear. They take little changes and turn them into large effects. The butterfly wing effect, in other words. Designing an innovation opportunity means understanding the system itself, the people who use it, and the external landscape in which that system exists.

So how do we come to terms with all this complexity and non-linearity? With a few cognitive shifts. The first one is to **forego any hope of ever really predicting outcomes**. Foresight and planning for innovation should be an exercise in probability and never prediction. Believing otherwise is a set-up for failure. Having abandoned the hope of prediction in favor of probability, the next cognitive shift requires that we **embrace uncertainty** and use scenarios to build resilience and agility into our ideas and our innovations. Like building a back porch or upgrading your home, smart organizations use scenarios to guide their innovation through adversity and discontinuities. Typically, these take the form of a positive linear scenario, business as usual with steady growth. With the positive non-linear scenario, things get way more optimized much more quickly than expected. Then there is the negative linear scenario; things get steadily worse. And lastly, a negative non-linear scenario; the system crashes into chaos.

Counterintuitivity · making meaningful innovation

The third shift requires that we **learn to think in terms of systems** rather than parts. One of the most underrated skills, in my opinion, is systems-thinking; thinking beyond the visible edges; and wrapping our heads around non-linearity, while understanding where impacts and shifts may happen. Not to predict these, but to understand the likelihood of what influences and alters something else. If that's too hard, we can offload the effort to machines. Computing helps the models edge closer to offering more probability of likely outcomes.

As has been said, you may not be able to predict the future, but you can build it. The best way to manage the vast probability field is to collapse it into a reality of your own construction. Foresight and futurism are activist pursuits. For all our focus on futurism as being about the future, it's actually a lens on the present, a snapshot of the way we deal with time itself and how we prioritize our actions. A strategic forecast will challenge us to act proactively. Systems-thinking calls to the heart and spirit with visions of how things might come to pass if our will is strong enough, or too weak. In times of global change and shifting paradigms, all organizations should be embracing systems-thinking to evolve and adapt in the dynamic environment. But that first requires senior executives to recognize and understand when they are stuck so that they can stop digging the hole of obsolete strategies.

11 Stop digging deeper holes

Counterintuitivity · making meaningful innovation

PART 3 • ACTING ON WHAT MATTERS

chapter 12
Inner Work Lives Matter

DO YOU EXPERIENCE meaning while at work? Most likely, you are working at, or for, a company that aspires to greatness. A corporation that articulates a high purpose through its corporate mission statement. Or maybe through a strategy that sets an inspirational vision for the future. Most brands do this, and its leaders and management are there to embody the mission and vision. Perhaps you are one of those managers. Could it be that you are inadvertently signaling the opposite of that vision through your words and actions?

Of all the variables that can deeply engage people in their jobs, the single most important is making progress in meaningful work. Even incremental steps forward—endearingly called the low hanging fruit—boost what I call "inner work life": the constant flow of emotions, motivations, and perceptions that make up a person's reactions to the events of their workday. A day of rich interactions between other people where each of these interactions has an influence on how the day is experienced. Sometimes it is as tangible as

12 Inner work lives matter

delivering a 'bad day' at work, other times it is offering you a renewed sense of belonging and a re-energized drive for the next day.

It's clear as day; people are more creative, productive, committed, and collegial in their jobs when they have positive inner work lives. The first and fundamental requirement is that the work must be meaningful to the people doing it. That it gives them a sense of belonging, accomplishment and feeling that it holds their voice.

Fact: senior executives often routinely undermine creativity, productivity, and commitment to innovation. And they do so with the best intentions of trying to avoid just that. They may think developing a killer strategy is their main job. In fact, this is only the first job. There is a second, equally important job: enabling the ongoing engagement and everyday progress of the people in the trenches of your organization who strive to realize and deliver that innovative vision. To do that successfully and consistently requires more leadership qualities than managerial ones. This "second job", to see meaning anchored within innovation, upholding its vision to keep engagement and momentum among those who are involved, is, in my experience, the more challenging work.

Notice I drew a distinction between leadership and managerial qualities. They are a polarity. There are differences (fig.7) between managing the circumstances, and leading outcomes beyond them. Both are needed. Management has a structured approach with the short-term aim for efficiency. It addresses, responds, and shapes for the partial; for someone. Leadership has an unstructured approach with a long-term view geared toward effectiveness. Leadership seeks to address, respond, and shape for the whole; for everyone. Management is directive and should bring stability. Leadership is transformative and aims to unify. It is through leadership that work-

Counterintuitivity · making meaningful innovation

ing relationships are shaped. Those interactions you have on a daily basis with colleagues and peers? These are each micro relationships.

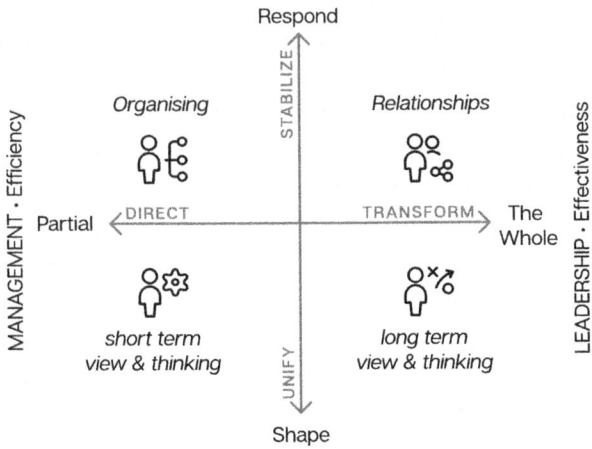

fig7 the roles of Managing for efficiency and Leading for effectiveness

Managers at all levels, in all industries (the creative ones included) routinely—and often unwittingly—undermine the meaningfulness of work for their direct subordinates through everyday words and actions. Simply by doing their managerial job of prioritizing efficiencies. These include dismissing the importance of an employee's thinking or ideas, or destroying a sense of ownership by switching people off project teams before work is finalized. Shifting goals so frequently that people do not know how their work will meet expectations. Delaying decisions such that the team fears the project will never see the light of day. Even neglecting to keep them up to date on changing priorities or new decisions.

It happens on an hourly basis, so common for most that it is invisible for us. Even the senior leadership in a company has unknowingly killed meaning at work, all while demanding it from their sub-

12 Inner work lives matter

ordinates. And this could simply be from not realizing that the role of managers is to enforce stability and organization. Which are two elements that are hard to come by when you explore new meaningful innovation. Granted, as a high-level leader, you have fewer opportunities to directly affect the inner work lives of employees as compared to line managers, team leaders, or supervisors. Yet a sense of purpose in the work, and consistent action to reinforce it, has to come from the top.

The intent may be just that; reinforce a sense of purpose in the daily grind of a working day. A company's leadership may be actively implementing important projects, doing what they think they need to do in order to get their companies across the finish line of a successful and meaningful innovation. Unbeknownst to them are four traps that lie in wait for them to fail at making it meaningful. Companies can get trapped in **mediocrity, strategic ADD, wrong metrics, and mis-coordination.**

An innovation that has meaning needs to have been designed and delivered by those who find it meaningful. It is a gift; for a brand or company to give the gift of meaning, its employees need to have that meaning first. I believe that it is possible for senior executives to sustain meaning consistently, but it requires vigilance. Without that, leaders risk falling into some of these traps themselves—and unknowingly dragging their team or organization into the abyss with them. If they want to begin changing that, they must first be curious about these traps.

I have seen this dynamic at well-known consumer products companies and financial services brands. A rapid deterioration in the inner work lives of its employees as a result of the actions of their top-management teams. For one of these companies it turned out catastrophically; it had become unprofitable and was acquired by a smaller rival. Their top-management team had adopted a vision of entrepreneurial cross-functional business teams. Inline with the theories of innovation, each team would operate autonomously, managing its share of the company's resources to back its own new-product innovations. Their annual report was full of references to the company's innovation focus; in the first five sentences, "innovation" appeared three times. In practice, however, those top managers were solely focused on cost savings and margin protection, and they repeatedly negated the teams' autonomy. They dictated cost reduction goals that had to be met before any other priorities were. As a result, while they gained efficiency, they drove new-product innovation into the ground. This obviously took its toll as exposed during interviews with several of its specialists: "It is getting very difficult to concentrate on removing pennies from the standard cost of an item," said one. "We are no longer the leader in innovation. We are the followers," lamented another. All signs that for the employees at this company, work had begun to lose its meaning. Many other professionals in our research study expressed they, too, felt that they were doing mediocre work for a mediocre company—one for which they had previously felt fierce pride. By the end of our time collecting data, it was evident that many of these employees were completely disengaged. They felt trapped in **mediocrity**.

The mediocrity trap was not unique to this firm alone. I saw it revealed in different guises in several of the companies that engaged consultants to help with their innovation efforts. At a chemicals firm, it stemmed from the top managers' risk aversion. A proposal for an innovation using their own new technology was tabled for the second time by their own committee. Although we had plenty of evidence-based insights and a creative idea that had the working team excited and proud, the committee declared its discomfort with

12 Inner work lives matter

the risk and the unknown of this new idea. The criteria of the vision the company was not met with the willingness of its management to live by them. Despite their rhetoric about being innovative and cutting edge, they were really more comfortable being ordinary and unremarkable. For the management of this self-proclaimed industry leader, mediocrity was enough to save their jobs. However, it proved insufficient for their talent to stay committed. Theory would have it that an experienced leader would scan their company's external environment constantly for guidance in deciding their next strategic moves. They would try to understand what competitors are planning. Where new ones are popping up. What's happening in the global economy, and what might the implications be for financing or future market priorities. All of that is good, in theory.

However, in practice, too many top managers start and abandon initiatives so frequently that they appear to display a kind of attention deficit disorder (ADD) when it comes to strategy and tactics. This is the second trap where innovation gets stuck; a lack of determined focus. They don't allow sufficient time to discover whether initiatives are working, and they communicate insufficient rationales to their teams when they make strategic shifts. Sometimes not even recognizing that they are making such shifts. **Strategic ADD** could be happening because of a management's desire to embrace the latest innovation trends. I see evidence of this problem in decisions at the level of product lines. If you blinked, you could miss the next strategic shift. On one program, a quarterly review was held with members of the innovation team, the general manager and president. Primary outcome from the meeting was a change in direction. Four new priorities were defined for product development, none of which were identified as priorities at our last quarterly update. No clarifications were provided; the top had decided this was to be done in the new quarter. For them, the needle still points north, but to the team, it seemed they've turned the compass again. Which inevitably signals that their leaders don't appear to have their act together on exactly where the organization should be heading. It's awfully difficult for employees to maintain a strong sense of purpose under these circumstances.

Every design and innovation requires a measure of success. A target or metric that can have its success made evident. However, sometimes, targets and metrics are bad for business. The third trap to erase meaning out of your innovation effort: **wrong metrics**. The never-ending quest to quantify innovation can go terribly, terribly wrong. Our value as employees is often boiled down to the quantifiable.

But there's a problem with that: When a metric becomes a target—that is when it becomes the primary focus of a job—it ceases to be effective. It then only becomes a measure of efficiency. Something to manage. Doing only what is efficient is a friend to neither meaning nor innovation. When a company is not focused on measuring what actually matters it will result in missed opportunities and meaningless work. The promise offered by emerging technology trends like big data and cloud-based analytics promise to help executives develop greater insight into their businesses, allowing them to transform and innovate, thus heralding a new era of productivity gains. A major issue among firms is that many of the business performance reports they develop are looking in the rearview mirror when they should be more focused on the road ahead. Once the firm has identified the most important reports to focus on, it should ensure that they always first consider the data points necessary for business forecasting. All while avoiding "vanity metrics." You certainly shouldn't let your attention be distracted by reporting on the numbers that paint the rosiest picture. Business relies heavily

12 Inner work lives matter

on numbers, but far too often, businesses focus solely on the immediate impact or efficiency of innovations, rather than waiting to see them through to the end. Impatient organizations often kill plans or ideas far too soon, before seeing them to fruition, which not only is a waste of company resources, but strikes a dangerous blow to a company's innovative culture. Big businesses need to broaden their scopes so that the numbers fixate not just on immediate impact, but also concentrate on long-term or market-growing innovations.

In the early decades of cinema, the era of silent films, a popular comedy series was the Keystone Kops—fictional policemen so incompetent that they ran around in circles, mistakenly bashed each other on the head and fumbled one case after another. I'm often reminded of this when I witness many executives who think everything is going smoothly in the everyday workings of their innovation project, blissfully unaware that they run their own corporate version of the Keystone Kops. It's the fourth trap for innovation to get bogged down in; **mis-coordination.**

Some leaders contribute to it through their actions, others by a lack of it. For some, it is the set-up of overly complex matrix reporting structures, that repeatedly fail to support coordinated decisions needed to push forward with their innovation. For others, it is experienced as a chronic indecisiveness that breeds rushed analyses and uncommitted, delegated suggestions, that get presented as a decision. I recall the attempts of a team to move forward with their projects continually halted because, despite attempts, the management of a partner department failed to show up for many key meetings. The mixed signal and lack of coordination and support saw people stop believing that they could produce something of high quality. This makes it extremely difficult to maintain a sense of purpose.

Counterintuitivity · making meaningful innovation

With another group, there was a strange hierarchical dynamic, where the project owner was outranked by the assistant project owner. This confused a number of people in understanding who owned the final decision or whose direction to adhere to. It didn't help that both had different reporting lines, with the product owner's (PO) boss now outranking the assistant PO. Numerous starts and stops were the result, where the team had to reset and rally toward changing visions, priorities or even KPIs. When you don't know where you are going, any road will do. Hence a majority of the team was on different tracks, aiming for different things. Soon to realize that none of it was of meaning. If somebody asked you to do a bunch of work on something they hadn't thought through, how meaningful could it be for you? How committed would you be?

Spotting the traps from the executive suite is difficult enough; sidestepping them is harder still—and it is never the focus of an innovation project. Nonetheless, it's instructive to raise your awareness in order to avoid the traps and create conditions that are conducive for bypassing these altogether. When leading innovation, your challenge is to help your organization, and the teams involved move appropriately, depending on context and shifting priorities. To address the inner work of those under your care, as a leader, you must constantly ask yourself "How will I affirm each person's need for individual contribution yet also tend to the needs of the collective?" "What can I do to encourage team members to support one another while simultaneously challenging and provoking each other through robust debate?" "How do I champion continuous learning and high performance?" "Mix patience and a sense of urgency?" "Allow bottom-up initiatives and respond to top-down interventions?"

Managing these paradoxes will inevitably depend on specific current circumstances and context. The goal will always be to en-

12 Inner work lives matter

able the collaboration, experimentation, and integration necessary for innovation. This kind of leadership is not easy, especially for leaders who hold conventional notions of top-down leadership, or who find conflict or loss of control uncomfortable. Even skilled leaders of innovation find it hard not to favor one side of the paradox scales over the other. They must develop the capacity to lead from the right place on each scale for the moment and situation.

What both managers and leaders can activate is engagement; the right kind at the right time for the right people. If ever it was as easy as writing that! There is a distinction between communicating with one person, or with many. But by and large—and I ask forgiveness if this sounds generic—managers and leaders either seek to (fig.8) **instruct, inform, involve, or inspire**. Be it individual or groups of individuals. When you seek to instruct or inform others; the more successful way of doing this is with a low-emotional connection. Facts and figures kind of stuff. Policy. When you aim to have people feel involved or inspired, a much higher emotional connection is needed. Now take a moment and account for the quality of communications you either make or receive in order to instruct, inform, involve or inspire.

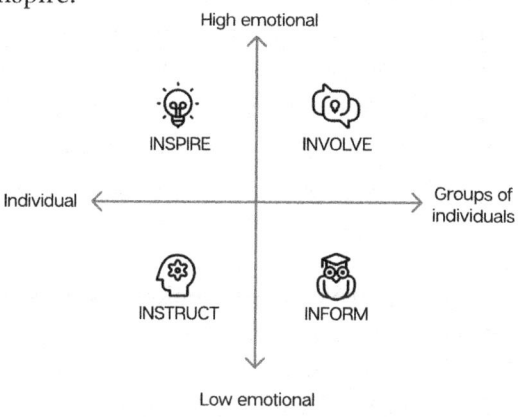

fig.8 The Engagement Continuum

Counterintuitivity · making meaningful innovation

Need to communicate strategic clarity with employees consistent with your organization's capabilities and provide an understanding of where they can add the most value? Low-emotional or high-emotional? Or a better question would be; which part is low, and what is better done with a high-emotional connection? It is the right combination of both, and that only works when there is enough visibility and understanding of who the individuals are that make up the audience of your message.

Do you have an ear on the ground? A sort of early-warning system that indicates when your view from the top doesn't match the one below? Spending time to understand what people's personal interests or motivations are toward the work they are asked to do will bring attention to what can start to sap meaning from their work. Investigate to identify and clear away systemic impediments that prevent quality work from getting done. You can provide a sense of purpose and progress by just making that effort. What are the obstacles to better performance? While you are doing this, can you keep sight of the individual employee's perspective?

As an executive, you are in a better position than anyone to identify and articulate the higher purpose of what people do within your organization. Make that purpose real. Work to make it land for those asked to rally around it. When they rally, support this through consistent everyday actions, and you will create the meaning that motivates people toward greatness. Along the way, you may find greater meaning in your own work as a leader.

Leaders, in essence, are meaning-makers. Now, what if you are not a leader? What if you don't (yet) have that appointed position, yet are committed to a meaningful contribution in creating innovation? How can you position yourself as being of influence, ready

12 Inner work lives matter

to offer creative thinking or actions that advance innovative ideas? To do this, one part of the answer is mindset, the other purpose. A majority of us still see expertise and experience as the same, and for most, purpose is to be built and not something you find as a result of looking for it.

The first door to kick in; expertise and experience are not related. Certainly not as strong as we may have come to believe it. Despite appearance and a false sense of logic, one does not result in the other. It is not because you have years of experience that you are an expert. You are merely experienced and have learned from exposure to something. Experience means you've done something a lot. Should the people who've been in a job the longest be paid the most and be seen as the leader or expert?

This is still the way many businesses work, regardless of industry. I see the same practices within creative and consulting services. Employers pay their staff an annual increment based on their years of employment even if the role hasn't changed. All because of our belief that experience "counts." Hence, the longer you do the job, the more you should be paid. The more you are paid, the more we see experience as a form of expertise. That is the false logic; doing the same thing long enough to be rewarded for it adds points on the expertise scoreboard. It shouldn't be that straightforward. What if not everyone was making their experience count?

By all means, you can only become an expert with experience. Just that experience alone does not make you an expert. Experience simply marks the time we do something, but it's a bad gauge of how well we actually do it. In his book, Peak, Anders Ericsson unpacks research that reveals performance can actually decline with experi-

Counterintuitivity · making meaningful innovation

ence. Why is this so? How come experience counts for some people but not for others?

Because it's not the time on the job that counts. It's how you spend the time. Those who build their abilities and become experts spend a great deal of time engaged in either deliberate practice or purposeful practice, both leading to growth and making future growth possible. This is, in other words, a form of inner work. We are each afforded the same amount of time in a day. How we use that time to enhance our capabilities is our individual merit. It's what shapes expertise. Experts are practitioners. If you embrace the practice of expertise, your aim is to extend your abilities. That involves willingly and knowingly stepping outside your comfort zone. That is uncomfortable. In fact, the discomfort would be a sign you are doing it right. Shaping expertise is highly focused and is guided by specific performance measures. Importantly, both a deliberate and a purposeful practice is characterized by mistakes that guide future learning. People who fail to develop expertise with time tend to naively believe this will lead to growth, but it doesn't.

If you use repetition and rehearsal and performing tasks that have already been mastered as a path to expertise, you are, in fact, not moving forward. You are treading in place. Meanwhile, the world is moving forward, changing, evolving. This means that you are actually not treading in place as much as you are falling behind. It could still feel as if you are working hard, but the work is done in an unfocused and undirected way. This sort of practice is, at best, inefficient. At worst, it's failing to create personal growth. Increasing the distance toward arriving at expertise.

This raises the interesting idea that—from the perspective of your future self—you are under-performing. When expertise is a

12 Inner work lives matter

growth toward better capabilities and newer abilities, you need to be stepping up your performance. If you're capable of a much higher level of performance, why aren't you operating at that level now? And, more importantly, how do you achieve that higher level of performance? What's your true potential? The reason you can't simply start performing at your future self's level now is that you don't have the brain for it. Your current brain isn't wired the same way as your future brain. This means those future abilities are beyond your current potential.

An expert practitioner understands this and therefore looks for that which will see their brain rewire itself in new ways, creating new abilities, deepening their knowledge while expanding their range of possibilities. The practice to expertise, as per Ericsson's recommendation, requires Focus, Feedback, and Fixing. Simply working hard doesn't work. You need to focus on improving on small, specific skills. This allows you to target specific parts of your brain for rewiring and to create effective change. Taking a directed, purposeful approach to what it is you want to improve on is key. With every attempt, you'll get closer to creating change. Getting specific feedback about what went right and what needs to be corrected is vital to this process. Ideally, this feedback comes from an expert, someone who's done it before and knows exactly what steps will lead you to growth. If there's no expert available, then there must be a clear set of standards about what you aim to achieve. Armed with feedback and a focus on what you need to change, you must then go back and modify your actions to get it right. Or to get even better. This means re-entering the process of focus, feedback, and fix it again and again. It's important to do this until the process results in new connections in the brain. Only then will new abilities be formed. Only then are capabilities widened.

Counterintuitivity · making meaningful innovation

A few years ago, September 20 2014, one of my guitar heroes, Joe Satriani[47], visited Singapore (where I currently live) for a concert. This was to be his first gig there. For me, it was a first to see this virtuoso perform live, in person. In a bucket list moment for me, I had an opportunity to meet him and have a chat. Being a hobbyist guitar player, and one who has a love-hate relationship with the instrument, I confessed to Joe that I sometimes find it difficult to stay motivated and committed to playing. And, offering a moment of vulnerability, I expressed how I sometimes felt futile in wanting to master this instrument. The sly smirk on Joe's face underscored that this was certainly not the first time he heard this confession. With that, he replied,

> "Your problem is that you want to beat the instrument. You want to master it, conquer it. You can't because you're not supposed to. I don't consider myself to be done with the guitar. And I wouldn't want to. I just want to spend a focused amount of time with it. My instrument and I are in agreement with what we should do together."

Joe helped me understand that practice alone isn't a way of reaching my potential; it's how I practice. Even practice can be an act of creation, not just repetition. We each create our own potential. We are limited only by our opportunities to engage in our practice. Practice and rewiring your brain takes time. There are no shortcuts because there is no finish line. The practice is never done, there is no end game. That's why you can only achieve expertise with experience. Expertise takes experience—but it must be the right sort of experience. Your experience does not reflect your expertise and if you want to accelerate your career, feel engaged with the work you do, you need to focus on developing expertise. And because this is a type of inner work, expertise is a mindset more than it is a skill set.

---

[47] www.satriani.com/ and https://twitter.com/chickenfootjoe

12 Inner work lives matter

Hand in hand with the development of expertise is the construct of purpose, the second part to the leadership equation. Often advised as something you need to go look for, purpose is to be built. Working with a sense of purpose day-in and day-out is an act of will. It's an act of self-management that takes thoughtfulness and practice in order to do. Having observed friends and colleagues working with and without purpose for years, I'd offer the one thing that helps to consciously deliver your work with purpose—regardless of your profession or role within an innovation project.

Why?

It's a question all of us should ask ourselves. Why do we do what we do? In particular, why do we do the work that, for many of us, occupies most of our waking hours for our entire adult lives? Ralph Waldo Emerson left us a quote worthy of one of those inspirational wall posters: "The purpose of life is not to be happy. It is to be useful, to be honorable, to be compassionate, to have it make some difference that you have lived and lived well." That thought may feel warm and fuzzy, but the question remains: Why do we do the work we do? I believe it is by understanding the bigger picture and connecting work to service. The engagement with what we do at work will deepen when we know that everyone involved in the innovation effort is there to serve someone in what we do. That is not unlike teachers who can see the young lives they are shaping every day—and visualize the lasting impact they may have on the young lives they touch. Who do you serve? Connecting our day-to-day jobs—consciously and concretely—to those we're ultimately serving makes crafting and completing that work more purposeful. It crafts the meaning into it.

Counterintuitivity · making meaningful innovation

Speaking of craft; craft your work—and make work a craft. Just by seeing the work on hand as a craft, and not a job, something interesting happens in how we feel about it. A fascinating new study took an in-depth look at how custodial staff understand and feel about their work. The study uncovered wisdom for finding a sense of meaning in work. Amy Wrzesniewski[48], now a professor at the Yale School of Management, had the radically simple idea of talking to the custodial staff at a hospital to discover what strategies they might employ to find satisfaction in their admittedly low-skilled, low-paid jobs. The wisdom she uncovered should serve to humble anyone who has ever made the error of thinking of those who work in the profession with condescension.

Wrzesniewski uncovered a practice among the happiest and most effective custodians she termed "job crafting." That doesn't mean changing your work, it means carefully crafting how you think about your work as to go beyond what is expected from it. These custodial workers, focused intensely on serving patients, would "create the work they wanted to do outside of the work they'd been assigned—work they found meaningful and worthwhile." One would rearrange artwork in rooms to stimulate comatose patients' brains; others devoted time to learning about the chemicals they used for cleaning rooms and figuring out which were least likely to irritate patients' conditions.

I recall a story that Steve Wynn, the founder of Wynn Resort & Casino, shared of his family's trip to Paris. This was a few years ago. He had dropped his wife and adult daughter off in Paris and then flown on to Singapore. They were staying at a Four Seasons Hotel George V, just off the Champs-Élysées. Where, one morning, they ordered breakfast in their room. The daughter, Gillian, only

---

[48] Publications by Amy Wrzesniewski https://som.yale.edu/publications/faculty/amy.wrzesniewski-at-yale.edu

12 Inner work lives matter

ate a half of a croissant, but because she felt it was delicious, she left the other half for later. They then left to explore Paris. Upon returning to the hotel room, the pastry was gone. Gillian was disappointed and assumed housekeeping got rid of it. An honest assumption; that would be what housekeeping is asked to do. On their room telephone, however, there was a message from the front desk. Informing them that housekeeping had indeed removed the half-croissant from the room, assuming that upon arrival, they would prefer a fresh pastry. So the front desk contacted the kitchen to set aside a croissant, and room service was ready upon request to deliver the fresh pastry. The level of teamwork and communication between different departments in the hotel was simply magical. All participants understood the end result—customer satisfaction. And everyone accepted their role in making the experience fantastic.

Both the custodial workers and the hotel staff were pursuing excellence in service to others and would adapt their jobs to suit that purpose. They enhanced their assigned work to be meaningful to themselves and to those they serve. This focus on crafting their work into something that gives them purpose while still getting the core of their job done ultimately made the work a lot more meaningful for them. This crafting is also a demonstration of treating work as a practice—focusing on the skill needed to complete one's work and dedicating oneself to perfecting those skills. This atmosphere of constant improvement in service of craft in itself seems to fill professional pursuits with greater purpose. This implies we have to let go of our addiction to being right. We have been rewarded for being right, but that won't work here. Having answers blocks insight and perpetuates biases. Aiming to know results in closing curiosity. Instead, we should focus on building a mind for growth, not certainty.

Consider also that who we work with is as important as what we do. Psychologist Martin Seligman[49] has written extensively on the importance of relationships to happiness and fulfilment; the now famous Harvard Grant Study[50] found that happiness and even financial success are tied to the warmth of one's relationships. While relationships necessarily and appropriately look different within the workplace than outside of it, they still matter. We'd all be served by identifying more ways to develop positive collegial relationships at work. Whatever your approach, efforts to enhance the positive relationships you have with others at work—often investing in serving them—can give work greater meaning. Your results are shaped by what you pay attention to. What you pay attention to is ultimately your business, but it should be a conscious choice.

Although creativity is spontaneous in nature, it requires a degree of passion. A willingness to share, express, improve, or resolve. Guiding this passion and bringing people to willingly share their degree of passion is an important role of the design or innovation leader. When they take time to understand what is required as clarity and condition to have creativity arise more easily, they will soon appreciate just how rich the minds of other people are. That richness needs guidance, it is still required to direct minds in a particular direction so that relevance is part of the ideas and thinking. That is the layer that a leader can bring on top of the creativity that was purposefully incubated within the teams they work with.

Purpose isn't magic—it's something we must consciously pursue and create. Discovering a sense of purpose and acting on it should be free of expectations. Not even conceiving or aiming at

---

[49] Profile https://www.authentichappiness.sas.upenn.edu/faculty.../profile-dr-martin-seligman
[50] https://www.health.harvard.edu/mind-and-mood/positive_psychology_in_practice

12 Inner work lives matter

a goal. Purpose sounds fuzzy at first. Because purpose begins with finding clarity around intention. It doesn't have to be a lofty declaration; purpose could be as simple as being truly present in the next moment. And the next. Whatever the purpose you gravitate to, you need to put it into practice. Otherwise it is just more thinking, but in a mind that is not yet open enough for others to get a sense of meaning from you. That happens when you are more interested and aware about the process of being purposeful rather than the end goal you have directed yourself toward.

With the right approach, almost any job can be meaningful. If we are to deliver meaning in innovation, it is only possible by doing the work meaningfully. If we don't, then what is the point of innovation? Why do we focus so much time and effort on digital transformation, agile transformation, and innovation? Simply put, it's because large organizations need to grow—and can't. All of their current management practices are, perhaps unknowingly, geared to resist anything new ever being embraced as meaningful.

Counterintuitivity · making meaningful innovation

PART 3 • ACTING ON WHAT MATTERS

chapter 13
It's About To Get Emotional

THERE IS A pedestrian crossing just outside my condominium. My residence is located in the South West area of Singapore where we enjoy rapid access to two major traffic arteries as well as convenient transits using the public transportation. We have a bus stop on both sides of the main road, and as such we are required to cross the street on several occasions if we want to take a bus to go shopping at the nearby mall, or for my son to head to school. I'm not a fan of using the pedestrian crossing. Because it is not marked by a zebra pattern, running in a slow bend of the road, and with the traffic lights at a distance from where you are asked to cross, it is a low-visibility crossing. It doesn't help that the side of the streets has large trees, almost camouflaging us. During daylight, those unfamiliar with the area are often surprised by pedestrians crossing the road there. I know this because I have seen several drivers blow the red light. I have had to hold back my son to prevent him from being clipped by a car.

13 It's about to get emotional

I know this. I anticipate this. Which means that every time I approach this intersection with the intent to cross there, I am preparing myself. I am, without conscious knowledge, preparing to avoid being hit. As I approach this intersection, my body is preparing itself. Cortisol, a stress hormone, floods my body. As does adrenaline, extra energy should I need sudden movement, but also a primer for my senses. My focus is sharp, and I block out much of everything else in order to perceive any threat that may not be beneficial to my well-being. My bronchial tubes open up, allowing more oxygen conversion in my lungs. That gets transported more quickly, because my veins relax, allowing smoother blood flow to my muscles. Blood gets pulled out of my digestive system, however, and that is what causes the tension and 'butterflies' of nervousness and anxiety. Those are all part of the physical preparation my body is constructing; it puts your body in the best condition to deal with what you think may happen. But something else is being constructed. An emotion is being prepared: **Anger**.

I need not tell you it is dangerous when someone driving a couple tons of metal nearly hits you. It's bad for you. It's bad for everyone. So as my body is constructing its physical preparation, my mind is embarking on constructing an emotional one. You see, contrary to how we think about experiencing them, our emotions are preparations for what we think will occur, and not reactions to what just happened. Just as we prepare physically for what we imagine could happen, we prepare—in parallel—emotionally. I predict and simulate the possibility of being clipped by a car. I prepare for the need to make decisions more quickly. I need the clarity of purpose of an emotion. To help me act, to help me communicate, and in this case; to help me live longer. Every time I approach the crossing, the visceral preparation is joined by an emotional preparation. I could be angry.

Counterintuitivity · making meaningful innovation

Our minds predict and simulate realities to enable our passage through it. Our memories are used to construct realities, and our senses are used to nudge their "truthfulness" in the moment. Our imaginations fill in the gaps, and our emotions can manipulate our specific actions. Everything is built. Emotions are constructed. You are preparing to be emotional because the situation demands it.

A lot of our waking hours are spent like this. Emotions erupt within our minds not because you are reacting to events, but because you are preparing for them. We often mistake reacting with feeling, and then label that as the emotional experience. However, each of us are architects of our own experience; we build our emotions in preparation for events that we anticipate or feel we can predict. This innate process of constructing our emotions to what we predict can happen is something we do at various points in our day. Because when things are predictable, we never have to question ourselves, or the things around us. Predictability eliminates surprise, it eliminates effort. When things are predictable and known, we feel a sense of control, security. We know our role, what to expect, and what is expected from us.

It's easy to imagine that emotion gets in the way of the most difficult decisions. Get rid of this cumbersome human artefact and surely people would be able to make cold, calculating choices in the most exacting of situations. Not so. Neuroscientists have long studied people with brain injuries that prevent them from experiencing emotions. But instead of being precise, ruthless killers, these people are paralyzed by indecision. Emotions underlie even the coldest of human calculations.

The truth is that when it comes to everyday choices—deciding what to have for your lunch, for example—it doesn't matter how

13 It's about to get emotional

much cold hard logic you bring to bear; these decisions are ultimately emotional. Even the detailed calculations like those involved in mathematics and machine learning are governed by the fickleness of human emotion. Thomas Guntz[51] at the University of Grenoble in France and a few of his colleagues, measured the changes in the emotional state experienced by chess players as they tackle increasingly difficult problems. Concluding that emotions do play a key role in how these players make decisions in their attempts to solve complex problems.

Their hypothesis[52] is that the rapid changes in emotion are an involuntary display in reaction to recognition of previously encountered situations during exploration of the game state. The players reconstruct a previous emotion around the pattern recognition of a past experience. And that plays a crucial role in the decision of potential moves. The way advanced chess players do this decision making is very different from the thought process beginners use. Over time, expert players learn to recognize patterns of play or positions of strength and weakness. This pattern recognition significantly simplifies the process of deciding on the next series of moves. Expert chess players do not consider all the pieces separately, they consider these in groups called chunks. Top players are believed to store up to 100,000 of these chunks in their long-term memory. When they play a game, or solve a chess problem, they transfer their chunks into short-term memory, where the decision making takes place. Interestingly, there is a well-known limit on the amount of information that humans can store in short-term memory.

Back in the 1960s, the American psychologist, George Miller[53], showed that we can store between five and nine chunks that way[54].

---
[51] Profile https://fr.linkedin.com/in/thomasguntz/en
[52] Multimodal Observation and Interpretation of Subjects Engaged in Problem Solving https://arxiv.org/abs/1710.04486

Beyond that, we are overwhelmed. So how do chess players manage 100,000 chunks when they can only hold a handful in their working memory at any one time? "They use emotion," says Guntz. When a player spots a chunk he or she has seen before, the emotion associated with it causes it to be brought to for further analysis or rejected as a bad option.

It provides a curious new way to think about our problem-framing or our decision-making. Emotions clearly provide some kind of indexing system that allows us to access certain memories more quickly, and then have it influence our decisions as well as our observation of the problem that prompted the memories. Understanding how that works and how it can be applied to creativity and ideation is of key importance to delivering meaningful innovation.

At this point, everybody knows emotional intelligence matters in the workplace. It has been two decades[55] since EQ became a cornerstone of managers' self-improvement projects. Meditation has broken into the C-suite. Alpha males and females extol the virtues of mindfulness. And still, we remain unsure about what to do with emotions while working. Because there are two aspects of emotions that make it hard for people to exercise their emotional intelligence. First, most people are still not completely clear about what emotions actually are. Second, even when we understand emotions conceptually, it can still be hard to deal with our own emotional states. Let alone those of others around us; the misunderstood colleague, filled with frustration, attempting not to show it; the executive wondering how to confront a team's lack of enthusiasm; the manager hesitating to confess his fears to a peer.

---

[53] Profile https://en.wikipedia.org/wiki/George_Armitage_Miller
[54] https://www.instructionaldesign.org/theories/information-processing/

13 It's about to get emotional

One moment we do not have enough emotion, the next we have too much. We want work to ignite our passion, but we don't want our passions to affect our judgment. We want cool heads and warm hearts—as long as they remain apart. I'd like to argue that it might be a symptom of a work culture that views emotions in ways that keep us struggling with them in the long run. But first; what actually are emotions? Emotions are interpretations of feelings. While in everyday speech, *"emotion"* and *"feeling"* are often used interchangeably, psychologists distinguish between them.

The feelings you have—what psychologists call affect—emerge from your motivational system. You generally feel good when you are succeeding at your goals and bad when you are not. The more deeply your motivational system is engaged with a situation, the stronger your feelings. The motivational system, however, is not that well-connected to the brain regions that help you to tell stories about the world. In order to make sense of what you're feeling, you use information about what's going on in the world to help you translate those feelings into emotions—emotions help to guide your actions by giving you explicit feedback on how well you are currently achieving the goals the motivational system has engaged. Often, that interpretation is easy. Like if you are crossing the street and suddenly have to leap out of the way of an oncoming car, it is clear that the strong negative feeling you are having is fear from nearly getting hit by the car. If a colleague compliments you on a job well done, it is obvious that the positive feeling you are having is pride.

But things are not always so clear. You might have a bad interaction with a family member before getting to work. As the day wears on, you may interpret your negative feelings as a frustration for the

---

[55] A Brief History of Emotional Intelligence http://www.emotionalintelligence-course.com/history-of-eq/

project you're working on rather than lingering negative effect from the events of the morning. This is known as "an open unit of work." Many people try to power through their negative feelings rather than attempting to understand them by closing that unit. It is a lost opportunity because your emotions provide valuable information about the state of your motivational system. Ignoring them is like driving around lost, not only refusing to ask for directions, but refusing to consult the map or the GPS, or even to look out the windshield. You will still be moving forward, but who knows where you will end up. Conversely, paying too much attention to your feelings is also bad. That's like staring at a Google Maps screen, without ever getting in the car: you won't get anywhere that way.

Being willing to understand your feelings will have two benefits in the long term. First, it will help you to discover some of the aspects of your life that trigger negative feelings. That is useful because you don't want to misinterpret your negative feelings and attribute them to something else. For example, you would like to be in a situation in which you can recognize when events in your personal life are spilling over into work and are causing you to feel badly about the work you do, or make judgments out of an emotion that is not relevant to the work or the decision on hand. One of the most meaningful insights I was given during a personal development course, was when my instructor reminded the class of participants that "you can only see what the emotion allows you to see." If you are annoyed, all you find are reasons to be annoyed. If you are sad, it heightens your awareness of what makes you sad. Being able to recognize the pattern and then distance yourself from it is very liberating and grounding. It's hard work and takes time to take effect. But it allows you the second benefit, which is going to help position your influence and sense of meaning to others. Because by understanding the sources of your own emotions, you will become

13 It's about to get emotional

more expert in understanding the people around you as well. Once you can better understand what emotions are, and where your own emotions come from, you'll have a much better ability to practice emotional intelligence.

This EQ ability is of meaning in our work place, because in that environment, emotions are seldom distributed equally. Emotions are often bundled with certain roles and judgment. Who gets to feel what? Consider hope and despair, confidence and concern, pride and shame, poise and agitation, vocal outrage and silent contempt. The former in each pair is usually assigned to, if not expected of, people in powerful and visible roles. The latter is consigned to those in less powerful and visible ones. "Be yourself" and "get a grip" are common ways we are nudged into those places, as both often translate into, "Feel and show more of what I expect you to."

This runs counter to the common belief that our emotions are what funnel us into different roles, and that by managing those emotions we make ourselves more suitable for certain assignments. Because emotions are preparations to events, and not reactions to them, our roles and job titles often elicit our emotions. That is most evident when we move on from one role to the next, and feel the emotions dissipate, only to see them capture our successor. Needless to say, such conditions, never explicit but respected by most, does not bode well for problem-solving, mutual understanding, and collaboration.

What is the purpose of these prescribed emotions? They are a lens to examine what purpose, and whose interests, those feelings may serve—what they enable, what they avert, who they protect—and what everyone, including you, gets out of them. It may be safety, righteousness, approval, achievement, or relief. It may be the illusion that everyone gets what they deserve. It may be the familiarity, if not comfort, of what we experience—within and around us. A sense of knowing our place and what it feels like. Interpreted that way—tied to ourselves in a role, in context, doing work—emotions can help us learn about and manage more than just ourselves. They give us hints about what keeps us in our place, how we may change places, and even what it might take to change the whole place.

This implies that innovation is not just a cognitive process. It's emotional. It requires doing something new or novel, and that can be scary because it requires the courage to enter the unknown, and it involves learning from experimental failures. Many of us learned as children that success comes from making no, or the fewest, mistakes. We learned that making mistakes equates to looking stupid. We also developed emotional defenses to protect our views of ourselves to protect our egos. Protecting our egos and fears are the two big emotional inhibitors of innovation.

How do we begin to see new things that others don't see? As importantly, how do we perceive reality more accurately—see what we do not usually see? How do we have the courage to explore the unknown? How do we create something new? We have to overcome our fears of failure in order to iteratively learn. We have to overcome our self-centred views of the world so we can perceive the world as it is, not as we believe it to be. We must be more open-minded and less emotionally defensive when our views are challenged by others or by new facts. We must reflectively listen in a nonjudgmental manner. And to do all of that, we absolutely have to manage our emotions and be emotionally intelligent about our and others' emotions since innovation is a team sport.

13 It's about to get emotional

Positive emotions enable and enhance cognitive processing, innovative thinking, creativity, and lead to better judgments and decision making. Research has also shown that negative emotions—especially fear and anxiety—have the opposite effect. Fears and anxiety in the workplace can take many forms, including fear of looking bad, speaking up, making mistakes, losing your job, or not being liked. All of us are insecure and fearful to a certain extent and in certain situations. We want to be liked. We want to be accepted by the team. We want to fit in. Organizations must confront these emotional enablers and inhibitors through leadership role modeling, culture, human development, and by implementing research-based processes that individuals can use to manage their egos and emotions. They must design their work environments to reduce fears, insecurities, and other negative emotions. Without overcoming fear and having courage, people won't fully embrace the hard parts of innovating: giving and receiving of constructive feedback; asking and being asked the hard questions; being non-defensive, open-minded, and intellectually curious; having the courage to challenge the status quo and disagree with a higher ranking person; and having the courage to try new things and fail. Innovation happens best when we reduce our fears and ego defensiveness thereby freeing our minds to imagine, create, connect, and explore the new and unknown with others in a non-competitive way. That happens best when people feel psychologically safe and trust each other. **It is all about emotions.**

The main benefit of a high EQ, or the goal of developing your emotional intelligence, is to better understand the people around you. This can help you to interact with them more effectively and to understand what they want. It can also help you understand people's motivations, which even they themselves might have trouble articulating. Emotions can reveal information that people can't directly tell you: their motivational system. This system communicates with the rest of the brain through the feelings it generates. These feelings are interpreted by the brain, and that leads to the emotions people prepare or anticipate to experience. There are three core aspects of motivation that can be read from the emotions people display: success, commitment, and orientation. Obviously, there are many other things you can learn to read from emotions, but as we are looking to create and enhance meaning in what we do for innovation, these aspects of motivation that you can assess from what other people are feeling offer a direct route to what is important.

Success refers to whether a person is currently moving toward goal satisfaction or has recently achieved a goal. Goal success creates positive feelings, and goal failure creates negative feelings. For example, when people display positive emotions like anticipation, happiness, or relief, they are signaling that they have had a success before that is reminding them to feel confident about their prospects for more success. When they display negative emotions like fear, anxiety, sadness, or disappointment, they are revealing that they have had a goal failure before and that they are now anticipating one.

Those who experience negative emotions consistently are those who will identify only obstacles and goal failures—they only see the glass half-empty. They work out of scarcity. This opens up an opportunity to talk with them about whether there is anything that can be done to expand possibilities. There is often a tendency to focus on generating positive emotions in the workplace. That, too, can be counter-productive; the more satisfied people think they are with their current situation, the less motivated they are to move forward and try new things. A little negative emotion reflects that people have goals that they have not yet achieved. It is a balancing act to

13 It's about to get emotional

offer a pleasant workspace for meaningful innovation with the importance of helping colleagues to strive toward unfulfilled aims.

Commitment is the degree to which people are engaged with a goal that is important to them. You can read a person's commitment from the strength of their reactions. When someone has a strong negative reaction to a proposal at work, for example, we often say that we have "touched a nerve" in them. What we have really done is place an obstacle in front of a strongly held goal. The strength of the reaction is hard for people to control because it is driven by the engagement of the motivational system.

When dealing with people in the workplace, strongly emotional reactions are a clear signal of a deep commitment to an issue. It can be quite difficult for people to separate their emotional reaction from the importance of the goal for them. Sometimes, that strength of emotional reaction is a benefit. The passion people show as they strive toward a goal can be contagious to others. However, in settings like decision-making or prioritization in which each party may not get what they want, strong emotional reactions may get in the way of a settlement.

Orientation is a bit more complicated than the other two aspects of motivation. The two motivational orientations are approach and avoidance, and they are supported by different subsystems of the motivational system. The approach system is engaged when people are trying to pursue potential positive outcomes. The avoidance system is engaged when people are trying to pursue potential negative outcomes. When the approach system is active, people experience positive emotions of happiness, joy, and fulfilment, and negative emotions of sadness, dejection, and disappointment. When the avoidance system is active, people experience negative emotions of fear, stress, and anxiety, and positive emotions of relief and calmness. One reason why orientation is important is that it is valuable to help colleagues match their motivational state to the real problems facing them in the delivery of a project or the development of something new.

Many people find the workplace to be stressful. It's not any different in the innovation labs of the world. Stress and anxiety are signals of avoidance motivation. So if people are stressed, there is something significant in their environment they are trying to avoid. If the workplace would benefit from having people strive toward positive goals, then it is important to help people shift their focus away from the negative elements driving their fear and to focus them on the desirable outcomes that can trigger their anticipation and ultimate satisfaction with their work.

It is easy to get caught up in other people's emotions. We are wired so that our emotions are contagious. If we see someone else being passionate about an issue, we may get energized as well. It is important to observe the emotions of the people around you in order to better understand their motivations. It is also important to observe your own emotional reactions because they are some of the most important pieces of information about your own motivational state.

We have come to regard emotions as assets while they are more like data. It explains why we focus on managing, exploiting, diffusing, or sanitizing them rather than staying with them long enough to discern their meaning. And when we do the latter, we usually interpret them as revealing something about their owners alone. Seeing emotions only as spillovers of someone's inner world gives us an awareness of them and yet offers limited insight. Not because we're

13 It's about to get emotional

neglectful or incompetent at managing them. Not because we're hopelessly human. It is because our emotions at work are more than echoes of our history, expressions of our virtues and neuroses, or shadows of our longings. While those always play a part, emotions are seldom ours alone. What you and I feel at work has as much to do with what we are doing, and what others expect of people in our roles—and If someone likes us—as it does with our own inner lives. We readily accept that work shapes how we act and how we see ourselves that we regularly experience how others' expectations subtly corner us. We rarely think the same may be true of our emotions—even our private ones.

What if emotions were another element in innovation's unwritten script, which our history merely prepares us for and our aspirations make us more willing to perform? What if the assumption that emotions are ours—alone—to be minded and managed made us more likely to miss delivering meaningful innovation? Think about the emotions involved in experiencing memories, surprise, or discovery. How about excitement, motivation or belief? We each have eight core human emotions: Enjoyment, surprise, fear, anger, anticipation, sadness, trust, and disgust. There are many more nuances to this spectrum, but by and large, these eight are the primary ones.

Then there are sixteen hardwired desires in each of us, shaped by our motives, fears, and pleasures. As defined by the theory of desire[56] from the late Dr. Steven Reiss[57], an Emeritus Professor of Psychology at the Ohio State University. The concept for this theory originated from the time when Reiss was hospitalized during the 90s. As he was being treated in the hospital, he was able to observe the devotion and hard work of the nurses who took care of him. As

---
[56] http://changingminds.org/explanations/needs/reiss_16_needs.htm
[57] Profile https://en.wikipedia.org/wiki/Steven_Reiss

he saw how the nurses loved their work, he began to ask himself questions about what gives happiness to a person.

From the questions "What makes a person happy?", "What makes another person happy?" and 'What makes me happy?", Professor Reiss started to search for answer to these questions in the field of motivational research. He found out that there was little emphasis and no analytical models for the structure of human desires. Following his recovery, he commenced his own series of studies about human desires. In his vigorous research, he found out that there are 16 essential needs and values he called "basic desires", all of which are drives that motivate all humans.

After conducting studies that involved more than 6,000 people, Professor Reiss came up with these 16 basic desires These desires are triggered by emotions, evoked by pleasure signals. It's primal, and it's powerful. It's hard to pin down why people do what we do, choose what we choose. The Reiss Model of Human Motivation helps to more deeply understand these sixteen desires that color human preference and drive meaning-making.

What we declare as meaningful, we experience as an emotion. From that perspective, 'user experience' or 'experience' design is a rather lazy industry term. It is overused, and ambiguous enough that for most of us, it would mean that someone feels good about what they just interacted with. Surely, what we innovate does not need to limit the way in which we respond to it! Why could it not be stirring up any other emotion—by design?

13 It's about to get emotional

Counterintuitivity · making meaningful innovation

PART 3 • ACTING ON WHAT MATTERS

chapter 14
Thinking Inside Out

GOVERNMENTS AROUND THE world spend huge amounts on research and innovation. The vast proportion of this takes the form of financial support for innovation projects and activities, through mechanisms such as grants, loans, investments, inducement prizes, and service contracts. Innovators require other forms of support to develop the resilience, skills, capabilities, and networks that will enable them to use this funding effectively. However, we still don't know enough about what kind of support makes the most difference to innovators at which points, and the best way to design and deliver these types of services.

Innovation is not disruption, it's a mindful evolution. Done right, it understands and expresses the soul of something. An object, a process, a system, a code. And to more effectively express that soul, it uses new technologies, contexts, approaches, or meaning. In view of the previous pages, and to risk restating the obvious, I have a peeve with the rhetoric of innovation as a marketing tactic—the idea that we must be constantly "reinventing" objects and experiences in

14 Thinking inside out

order to capture the imagination (read dollars) of consumers. My issue is that innovation became its own goal, no matter its contribution to form or function, and that's the kind of innovation that is meaningless.

Such as reinventing what doesn't need to be reinvented. I doubt to be an outlier in having become seasoned to the hype of startups that are "reinventing" laundry, lunch, or learning. However, I believe that innovation and reinvention are fundamentally different concepts. Modern marketing language may have conflated the two, but it is worth unpacking, what I believe to be the true value of innovation. And reclaim that word from the corporate or marketing buzzword-aganza collection.

What is the innovation's core benefit to the people who use it? What values does it hold that set it apart from another thing? An innovation practice seeks to discover or define those values and then to design in a way that elevates them, to make the soul of the thing more apparent and useful. From the inside out. When change emanates from that understanding, it creates true meaningful value for people. When change is applied from the outside in, it is meaningless at best.

What I am saying is that design innovation is actually the deepest layer of the design process, not some act of creation, me-too-ness, or "disruption"—regardless of whether this is the outcome for it. At the top of the product design process, you have the surface-level work of designing the interface—the visible manifestation of the design process in layouts, colors, styles, and interactions. Those that only focus on the top layer won't succeed because the underlying structure, function, and features haven't been considered thoughtfully and systematically.

Counterintuitivity · making meaningful innovation

When you craft the middle layer—designing the experience—you increase the success rate. Applying Design-Thinking to understanding the problem, goals, and users, and then designing the right set of features and architecture to meet those needs. There are plenty of products that do reasonably well by only addressing the top two layers. These are the 'dime a dozen' apps, or the cookie-cutter services, the unremarkable products.

But the products and companies that have true success, the ones we look to as revolutionary, those that introduce new meaning, are the companies that go one level deeper and design meaningful innovation. In this layer, they are **designing the opportunity**. Designing the opportunity means understanding the system itself, the people who use it, and the external landscape in which that system exists. By comprehensively looking at all three of these factors, one can start to identify hidden opportunities and gaps.

To design meaningful innovation requires systems thinking on the existing variables and dynamics as well as the emerging ones. Inside-out means starting here and first learning as much as possible about what's happening now and the scope of the current system. That means understanding not only the technical scope but also what problem the product is trying to solve, and who it's trying to solve that problem for.

The next critical step to design meaningful innovation is to maintain perspective, to look outside of your own context to see the broader changes, technologies, behaviors, and expectations in the world around you. Develop information habits that routinely expose you to new developments, not only in your industry but in indirectly related fields as well. The best innovations often come from applying an approach from one context in a new environment.

14 Thinking inside out

As you spend time getting to know the people, the system, and the landscape, your creativity will have gaps and opportunities arise that seem ripe for innovation. Work to tease out those opportunities with structured explorations of the internal and external dynamics you're identifying. For example, you can map affordances of new technologies to user needs, or do concept mapping and other strategic foresight exercises to help you conceptualize the future. From there, you can work to articulate the vision of how to best innovate and take advantage of those opportunities. What is the experience we're introducing? What needs does it serve? How will we strategically experiment and what metrics can we use to know if it worked? How does it intersect with the development of our existing products? This work is all about getting everyone aligned on not only the goals and vision but also the functional expression of how we get there.

Innovation requires developing pathways to change, and change is always hard. Design innovation isn't just about coming up with great product ideas, but also about managing the organizational impact of those ideas. At all times, we need to keep in mind those most affected by proposed changes and collaborate to find workable paths to transformation at the human level, not just the product level. At all times, experimentation needs to be strategic to be successful. It avoids seeing your vision end up on the graveyard of promising but abandoned experiments. Or, not any better, it becomes the "ongoing" experiment that continues to be iterated upon without a clear sense of whether it's successful or not. Strategic experimentation should be accompanied by a hypothesis that is being tested, a clear set of metrics (qualitative or quantitative) to gauge success, and a process for when and how you will evaluate that success. In other words, any experiment should yield insights and lessons learned.

Counterintuitivity · making meaningful innovation

This, again, positions the leadership opportunity to 'manage by meaning.' Steve Jobs has always been considered an anomaly in management; his leadership style was something to admire or to criticize, but definitely not to replicate. He did not fit into the frameworks of business textbooks: there was 'according to the book' management, and then there was Steve Jobs. But there is a reason his management style is seen as the exception to the rule. Steve Jobs navigated a continuum that is often alien to management: the creation of meaning for both his employees and the brand's customers.

Apple, with Steve Jobs at the helm, put people at the center. However, this did not play out in that he gave users what they wanted. In fact, Jobs went on record saying that users do not know what they want. It did not mean that he instilled a playful organization where ideas flew from the bottom up either. Apple's approach to innovation was people-centric, but not user-driven: **it did not listen to users, instead it made proposals to them**. And one only needs to hear narrations on Jobs's leadership style to recognize a vertical, top-down, often harsh, approach where he stood center stage. At new product launches, he, not the team, was the protagonist. For Jobs, design was not only beauty but also creating new meanings for users. We know customers do not buy Apple's products simply because of utility or functionality; people are even prone to forgive some of Apple's technical limitations in exchange for meaningful design—and the identity they get through it.

A stark piece of evidence for this is the current disappointing sales[58] results of the latest iPhone series; between an XR and an XS and the model it is supposed to replace, there is no visible difference. The new XR and XS are both better functioning phones, with more recent technology. But Apple's audience wants something that

---

[58] https://www.forbes.com/sites/ewanspence/2019/01/09/apple-iphone-xr-sales-cut-drop-supplier-revenue-warning-services/#d7f4f0b241c1

14 Thinking inside out

is visibly distinct. They want to be seen as holding the latest model more than wanting the comfort of knowing they have the latest technology. Even between the XR and XS, which have similar technology, there is no actual visible difference. No justification of the significant price difference between the models. These new iPhones offer no new meaning to those who are asked to replace their previous model with it.

What Steve Jobs understood was that people appreciate the person who creates a meaning for them to embrace. Jobs was constantly driven by the search for products that made more sense to people. And that obsession saw Apple become a champion in creating new product meanings: the iMac G3, released in 1998, with his colorful translucent materials inspired by modern household products, changed the meaning of computers from ugly soulless office objects to visible, centrepiece home devices. The iPod plus the iTunes ecosystem gave a new meaning in the world of music. The iPhone turned the meaning of smartphones from objects for business to objects of social entertainment—and status. And while these products were not necessarily best in class in terms of performance, nor new technology that had never been commercialized, Apple's products under Steve Job's management were each more meaningful to users.

I believe the reason behind this is that Jobs also offered meaning to his employees. It is well documented that Apple's employees worked hard on visionary projects, striving to meet targets and to satisfy their leader's maniacal attention to detail. Jobs infused them with a sense of mission. Apple had to leave a mark in the world of computing, improve people's lives, be bold, and of course, "think different." That belief gave Apple's employees rationale, culture, and an emotional dimension to the work they performed, and as such, that sense of purpose and meaning translated into the prod-

Counterintuitivity · making meaningful innovation

ucts people simply loved. A lot of Jobs' success is written off as the fortunes of a once-in-a-generation unique character and personality. And because of both the quirks and the notoriety of his persona, nothing to be considered as a role model or as repeatable.

The traditional management of innovation is rooted in analytics, engineering, and the social sciences. As such the focus is outside-in: ideas, features, and priorities are driven by what we hear, observe, and synthesize from the collected user data. I cannot say whether Jobs had disdain for these or not, however, I believe his mastery of meaningful innovation was the ability to connect culture and the humanities with a vision of what could impact and be meaningful for people. Not just users; people. The clues are in the interviews; Jobs once stated that

> "The only problem with Microsoft is that they absolutely just have no taste. They don't bring much culture into their product. Proportionally spaced fonts come from typesetting and beautiful books.[59]"

And in 2010, during his keynote[60] for the launch of the iPad, he said,

> "The reason we've been able to create products like this is because we've tried to be at the intersection of technology and liberal arts."

That was not hyperbole or fancy public relations speech; that was Steve Jobs sharing the secret sauce recipe. The secret sauce? It is not about giving people what they want, it is about telling people what they should love. It validates Apple's peculiar innovation process under Steve Jobs: Insights do not move from users to Apple but

---

[59] extract from a 1995 interview: https://youtu.be/EJWWtV1w5fw
[60] 2010 iPad keynote https://youtu.be/zZtWlSDvb_k

14 Thinking inside out

the other way around. More than Apple listening to us, it's us who listened to Apple. We listened because Apple was not about to reinvent something, but rather it was going **to reimagine it**.

Here's why user-centric processes alone will not get us past our current convention of innovation. It feels provocative to the wisdom that is declared around how to innovate in this device-led world. It cannot be the only convention that every innovation process needs to start by getting close to 'users,' observing them using existing products or services and use what we already know with what we didn't know we needed to know, as a way to understand their needs. It only drives iterative, incremental innovation that aims to validate the predictability of our choices. It does not question existing needs; it reinforces them into patterns.

If we want to make innovation meaningful again, we have to disagree with this approach. User-needs see us respond to a market need, it does not have us make a proposal about what could be meaningful to us, or what could help us find new meaning and purpose in what we do. It's up to you whether you agree with this perspective. I am not asking you to thumb your noses at the notion of user-centered design or innovation. But it is not the only way to design, and it is not a suitable way to re-imagine possibilities. Steve Job's Apple had this approach to innovation, and to how innovation was managed within the company. It is not a coincidence that Tony Fadell and Matt Rogers, both former Apple engineers, happen to be the founders and creators of Nest, a programmable, self-learning, sensor-driven, and Wi-Fi-enabled thermostat that looks like a piece of jewelry. The idea came when Fadell was building a vacation home and found all the available thermostats on the market to be inadequate, ugly, and ultimately meaningless. This motivated him to bring something better on the market. Thankfully, you do not have to be

Counterintuitivity · making meaningful innovation

an Apple alumnus to be able to innovate new meaning. Nintendo did not act on user-needs—should they have done so, they would have provided another powerful processing console, capable of running higher fidelity games. Instead, they listened to developers within the industry, to understand what they would find meaningful. It allowed Nintendo to redefine the game experience by introducing the Wii.

And just as with the iPod, the Nest and Wii were outside of the spectrum of possibilities of what people knew and did—they were not outside of what they could imagine and love. All it required was that someone made that proposition to them. Creating radical innovations is about making a proposal, putting forward a vision, a possibility—but not without relevance or beyond the reach of people's imaginations. These radical proposals are not created by chance. And they do not simply come from the intuition of a visionary guru. We hail Steve Jobs as such, but I doubt that he alone had the ability to shape the meaning of Apple's proposals. It is within reach of all because it comes from a very precise process and capabilities. This is where culture and humanities play an influence in shaping choices around the innovation. Enabling this process will see companies become serial innovators of meaningful proposals. Their non-user-centered proposals are not dreams without a foundation. And sometimes they fail. But when they work, people love them even more than products that have been developed by simply scrutinizing their needs.

Sure, today we can shop for anything, connect with anyone, and find just about any information. And with our mobile devices, we can do this anytime and anywhere. But for all these conveniences and connections, our general sense is that we feel less in control of our lives. I believe we need much more radical innovations that empower people with "digital agency," enabling them to take control of their health, wealth, and happiness in ways previously thought impossible. In my view, humans are still as inventive and innovative as ever. It is the system that supports, and the processes that guide us, that have become timid and risk-averse.

The highly productive innovation ecosystem that thrived in the late 20th century—a synergy across academia, government, and industry—is now proving to be broken. Given the vast challenges that face society today, this is a tragedy. Too many innovators and entrepreneurs think if they just find the right idea everything else comes easy. They have it the wrong way around. The idea is easy. The search and iteration for a value proposition and business model is hard. Because success is not decided by the idea. It's execution and scaling that are measures of success.

It may have gone unnoticed: I wrote "too many innovators and entrepreneurs" as being two different personas. I long thought you needed to be innovative to be an entrepreneur. Now I have a different perception. Entrepreneurs are the ones who make things happen. That takes focus, diligence, discipline, flexibility, and perseverance. Entrepreneurs can take an innovative idea and make it impactful. Successful entrepreneurs also take challenges in stride, adapt, and adjust plans to accommodate whatever problems come up. Because of these capabilities, entrepreneurs often have the capacity to contribute to innovation. However, leading an idea from origination all the way to manifestation (commercial or not) is entrepreneurship.

Now, I'm all for leaders who want to ramp up the energy of their colleagues to take more chances and challenge conventional wisdom. Entrepreneurs who embody the innovation culture are inspiring and visionary. But what strikes me about the organizations that

Counterintuitivity · making meaningful innovation

are genuinely innovative is that they rarely use the language of innovation to describe what they do or why they do it. As entrepreneurs unleash new products and services, introduce exciting new ways to do the stuff they've always done, or identify new markets in which to do business, they simply do what makes sense and what comes naturally. They change what needs to change because it's the only way they can achieve what they want to achieve. It's rarely innovation for innovation's sake, or in innovation's name. It's done so in the name of entrepreneurship; in the name of profit. Meanwhile, not all innovators are entrepreneurs, and don't need to be entrepreneurial in order to innovate.

Until recently, I thought that I was alone in expressing these concerns around the way we declare what is innovation and entrepreneurship. I found myself out of step with the current huge wave of excitement about social media and consumer web technologies and large investments in these technologies. But things are changing. An article[61] in The New York Times profiles entrepreneur and investor, Peter Thiel[62]—Facebook's first outside investor and a co-founder of PayPal. He contends that the culture of innovation in the country has been on the decline since the 1960s. Thiel points to universities as lulling us into a false sense of security that results in a society that is simply coasting. Looking for the lowest effort to incremental change. While everybody is applauding the innovations in digital technology, and their applications on our devices, Mr. Thiel asked a simple question; "Is it helping people to have a much higher quality of living?"

---

[61] https://dealbook.nytimes.com/2011/05/19/contrarian-investor-shuns-hot-idea-for-bigger-picture/
[62] Profile https://en.wikipedia.org/wiki/Peter_Thiel

14 Thinking inside out

He is not just knocking the competition, he simply has a visceral aversion to the market's infatuation with what is not meaningful but gets billed as amazing. I applaud people like Mr. Thiel on their courage to declare that the "Emperor has no clothes." As a society, we are collectively in a state of denial about the meaningful innovations that are essential if we are not only to survive but also to thrive in the 21st century.

Most corporations and legacy brands are scared by culture, arts, and the humanities. Because none of it can be measured or codified into processes they know. These processes are applying an abstract sense of measure and code to the employees of the company. Contributions depend on the person and the personality of that person. However, innovators are people before being innovators. Users are, too. We all have a personal vision of the world, painstakingly developed through years experiencing life. Why should an innovator forget about culture? Why should an entrepreneur ignore it? No method, tools, and process can give you the capability to create meaning, to create visions. Only your personal culture, that no one can imitate, can. It is what I feel is sorely lacking in the post-Jobs Apple; the tangible evidence that business and culture are not in contradiction, but rather they sustain and inspire each other. Imagine the possibilities if we start to consider this as a model instead of an anomaly.

Part 4
Creating meaningful innovation

"Normality is a paved road; it's comfortable to walk on. But no flowers grow on it."

—Vincent Van Gogh, Painter

Counterintuitivity · making meaningful innovation

PART 4 • CREATING MEANINGFUL INNOVATION

chapter 15
The 9 Principles of Counterintuitivity

THE MOMENT THAT "innovation" becomes just another leadership program, yet another consultant-driven management technique, one more piece of language that defines so much of business life, it ceases to be a positive force for change.

I fear that very dynamic is unfolding today with respect to a leadership aspiration that has become the Holy Grail for their business. That aspiration is "innovation." That same aspiration sees them assigning chief innovation officers, establish innovation labs, appoint teams, position strategies—even organize innovation days or trips. Hackathon anyone? But are these companies doing any actual innovation? I see more evidence that they use the word to market making a step-change when the progress and outcomes they are describing are, in fact, rather ordinary and underwhelming. This makes me think that the word "innovation" has outlived its need. Innovation is broken. What we call good innovation is not empowering people, it lets them be lazy.

15 The nine principles of Counterintuitivity

Ouch, that's gonna leave a mark! But do lean in and give this statement some consideration. What if we all stopped "innovating" and set our sights on something more meaningful and real? Faster horses. This is what user centricity would have informed Henry Ford if he had started by applying today's innovation process. We did not invent, and then innovate, the electric light by continuously improving the candles. Iteration kills new ideas.

So what if we all stopped trying to "innovate" this way—and started trying to have fun and really do something new? And what if we set ourselves a more basic (and more authentic) set of challenges as we look to the future? What difference are we trying to make in our field? What do we care about? How can we reimagine the sense of what's possible in our field? What can we do that no one else in our business can do? How can we deliver what we've always delivered, but in entirely new ways? How can we apply what we've always been great at to markets or customer segments we've never worked with?

If you try to innovate the same way everyone else tries to innovate, it's hard to imagine or claim that you'll be very, well, innovative. Our stories of innovation usually follow a simple, but common narrative. Someone gets an idea, a eureka moment, rigidly and single-mindedly figures out how to make it work and then instantly changes the world. Evidently, that is rarely how it actually happens. Because if it did, our world would be dramatically different already. Far more often, someone comes up with a great idea, but it is unseen, unheard, and unappreciated. Despite recent advances and an improved understanding of the innovation process, game-changing, meaningful offerings remain elusive. Existing innovation models are unrealistic, and often incomplete or inadequate to meet the intent of those who apply them. Emphasizing speed and efficiency over

Counterintuitivity · making meaningful innovation

deeper reflection and reimagining possibilities. We gloss over pitfalls and biases and focus so intensely on users that we neglect to see them as human beings. Just like ourselves. If meaningful innovation holds the power to reimagine the world, it requires those wanting to create it to re-imagine their practices and behaviors.

Leapfrog innovators are those with an ability to find and visualize a new view, unbound by legacy or heritage, or former technology systems, or anything that could be experienced as holding them back. They fearlessly create new expressions, new experiences; new meanings. A lot of what they are doing is counterintuitive to what we're led to believe is the path to innovation. It's often not what most of us would believe is the natural way to go about it.

It's these habits that are the catalyst for this book. Now, it's not a Webster-worthy word yet, but perhaps it can become a movement: **Counterintuitivity.** My premises that by countering the predictability of our thinking and doing, our conversation design and decision making, as well as the roles we give ourselves in the development of innovative ideas, we can better assess the opportunities and potential pitfalls of how we move these forward with more meaningful propositions.

We're masters of our own thoughts, slaves to our own emotions, architects of our own experience. It's a fact of life for a human being, and therefore the terms and conditions for developing meaningful innovation. I want our innovations to remain human. In fact, I want it to become more meaningfully human. Because as machines take our jobs and do them more efficiently, soon the only work left for us will be the kind of work that must be done meaningfully rather than only efficiently. Technology should be beautiful, useful, and invisible. As consultants, designers, and as a business, we value do-

15 The nine principles of Counterintuitivity

ing something worthwhile, something of meaning. That asks from us that we nurture deeper relationships with our peers and clients to enable that vision of meaningful innovation. The following principles offer an alternative to embed meaning into the ideas that spark innovation.

> These 9 principles are 'Do what is seemingly unnecessary', 'Make the ordinary unknown', 'Choose more boredom', 'Create moments of affinity', 'Dare to be a little ugly', 'Forget how to fear', 'Change is permanent', 'Decisions just are', and 'Remain incomplete and unfinished'.

Each are a selection of techniques, mindsets, and methods, based on my experience, my work, and the systemic approach that works for me. I cannot assume that these will for you, but I can suggest you can experiment with them, as per your own individual needs. There is no strict order to follow, but you'll find either references or explanations on the context for them. Some of those are successes, others are failures, all of them have helped me find my voice and purpose in the world of design and innovation, and even more meaningful, they have enabled me to elevate and include the creativity and thinking of those around me.

These various practices and mindsets can help bring meaning and breakthrough ideas to fruition. So that this meaning can offer possibilities outside the tyranny of profit. Counterintuitivity offers ways to cultivate new relationship models that allow us to share in the risks and the rewards of collaborative, meaningful design innovations. To do this, I propose that you see my admittedly rather subjective principles as invitations to rethink what our contribution to innovation could, or perhaps should, be. Now that we have a shared

Counterintuitivity · making meaningful innovation

understanding that it is all about emotion and enablement of our innate human capabilities to create, imagine, and love, all I ask is that you attend closely and read with new eyes, and a step back to gain perspective. It can get unorthodox, but I think that is okay. If nothing else, it offers pictures from different perspectives; something any designer, innovator, engineer, scientist or researcher should find of interest—and perhaps even of meaning.

Everything that we innovate needs to embody the core meaning that people could be seeking, or are ready to rediscover. Delivering meaning cannot be an afterthought. The desire to do so needs to be deeply embedded in a company's culture, its mission, its strategy, and the core values of its employees. Meaning needs to be part of the core intent of an organization, as well as the core intent of those involved in innovation.

Designing for meaningful innovation is not only beneficial for the user, but is also key for business success. Delivering experiences that get to the core of what customers really value means they will identify more deeply with the brand and form a stronger bond with it. Observe Patagonia approach to consumerism[63] or IBM's purpose toward Smarter Cities[64]. Rather than brief, transactional interactions with a product or brand, you will find interactions to be deeper and longer lasting.

Meaning is the guiding and driving force within each of us. It's what helps us value ourselves, and the products and companies we interact with. It elevates innovation to a higher level of maturity and strategic presence. And it helps deliver positive business outcomes. Without meaning, we are missing the heart of why we are innovat-

---

[63] https://crm.org/articles/patagonias-customer-base-and-the-rise-of-an-environmental-ethos
[64] https://www.betterworldinternational.org/innovation/smarter-cities-ibm/

15 The nine principles of Counterintuitivity

ing in the first place. No matter what industry we are in—whether we create products or services, whether we have an enterprise or consumer focus, and no matter what our role is—we have an opportunity to drive successful business results in a way that also positively impacts people's lives.

Regardless of whether you are a designer, product manager, marketer, or developer—I hope that you will allow your craft and your decisions to be guided by the goal of delivering meaning to others. Here are a few principles to give you a head start in this.

Counterintuitivity · making meaningful innovation

"Do What Is Seemingly Unnecessary"

· *Counterintuitivity Principle 1* ·

IT ALL BEGAN with a birthday. On Saturday, June 23rd, 2018, Peerapat "Night" Sompiangjai turned 17—a milestone most young people around the world would want to celebrate in style. His family had prepared a bright yellow SpongeBob SquarePants birthday cake and several colorfully wrapped presents at their home in a rural village in Mae Sai district, in Thailand. But Night wasn't rushing home that day. He was out with his friends, the other members of a local youth football team, the Wild Boars, and their assistant coach, Ekkapol "Ake" Chantawong. When their football practice ended, they raced through the rice paddies on their bicycles and up into the forested hills that lately had been blanketed in rain. Their destination: the Tham Luang cave, a favorite haunt for the boys, who loved exploring the nooks and crannies of the mountain range towering over Mae Sai. Once at the mouth of Tham Luang, they stashed their bikes and bags by the cave entrance. The team and their young coach had often ventured deep into Tham Luang, sometimes as far as eight kilometers, for initiation rites where they would write the names of new team members on a cave wall. In high spirits, they clambered into the cave with just their torches. They didn't need

15 The nine principles of Counterintuitivity

much else—after all, they were only planning to be there for an hour. They would not emerge until two weeks later. Back at Night's home, his family began to worry. His birthday cake sat untouched. Where were the Wild Boars?

Swallowed up by an unforgiving mountain and surrounded by darkness, the boys and the coach lost all sense of time. Fear, perhaps even terror, would no doubt have crept in. But they were nothing but determined to survive. Coach Ake, a former monk, taught the boys meditation techniques—to help them stay calm and use as little air as possible—and told them to lie still to conserve their strength. Outside the cave, a full-blown rescue operation was quickly unfolding. Authorities called in the elite Thai Navy Seals, the national police, and other rescue teams. Local volunteers also pitched in, soon joined by international ones.

At the start, no one really had any idea what to do. Officials brought whatever equipment they could think of—small water pumps, long pipes, knives, and shovels—but much of it was apparently unsuitable. They even tried drilling into the mountainside, desperate to find cracks into the cave system which they could squeeze into, and used drones with thermal sensors to try to locate the boys. For three weeks in June and July 2018, the fate of 12 young footballers and their coach, and their sensational rescue, made Thailand's Tham Luang caves the most reported place on Earth. A small makeshift town mushroomed at the rural country park by the cave entrance. Food stalls were set up—some staffed by members of the Thai royal kitchen—serving free drinks, hot noodles, chicken rice, and even ice lollies. The country park toilets were dirty and stretched beyond capacity—so people began cleaning them voluntarily. Workers needed to get up and down the mountain—so drivers offered free lifts. Rescuers were covered in mud—so a local laundromat cleaned their clothes every night. Rice farmers gave up control over their paddies and allowed the fields to be flooded with the pumped-out cave water—effectively giving up their income. What happened is a remarkable story of friendship, human endurance, and the lengths some people will go to save someone else's child. It showed how uncertainty, unpredictability, and a lack of control had us see and experience renewed meaning.

"IT'S TIMES LIKE THESE YOU LEARN TO LIVE AGAIN. IT'S TIMES LIKE THESE YOU GIVE, AND GIVE AGAIN"

Dave Grohl — Rock n' Roll God

Working in or for innovation projects, our processes are geared toward us being more in control, but we can also allow ourselves to be less in control. We prioritize to act only on the necessary, but we can also opt to act on what is seemingly unnecessary, or unneeded. Something we couldn't control and have to let happen. Doing so may be wonderful moments to counter the predictability of our work, our decisions, and our designs.

I recall failing to act on such a moment. Years ago, when leading my own Shanghai-based studio, I was contracted to work on a branding project for an international merger of a large firm and a smaller firm. We were merging engineers with creative types. And to unify these immensely different cultures, the idea was to design and launch a new brand. I recall the new brand color was going to be yellow, Pantone P365. It had been a bit of a slugfest, the decision process had proven itself to be quite cumbersome. Without being

15 The nine principles of Counterintuitivity

aware of it, we had been cutting corners of the planned tactics, all in an effort to get this done and over with. As such, going through the budget for the rollouts, we made a last minute decision to cut the purchase of 10,000 yellow rubber ducks, which we had meant to distribute to all staff worldwide. Intended to bring a whimsical and light-hearted touch to this occasion, they now just seemed unnecessary and too unrelated in the end. We had no real idea how this distribution would play out—coordinating this appeared monumental. We felt out of control. The lesser effort was to simply abandon it, which we did.

It appears to me now that, in some way or form, that decision to abandon this tactic marked the beginning of the end—this merger eventually failed, the companies never became one. Now, was it because there weren't any yellow rubber ducks? No, of course not. But the kill-the-rubber-duck mentality permeated everything else. Prioritizing what was presumed the lesser effort meant the brand was ignoring what was needed. You might not always realize it, but when you cut out the unnecessary, you often cut out the meaningful. Innovating with meaning means rising above doing what is merely necessary. My advice to you? **Don't kill your rubber ducks.**

Question both the unnecessary and the obvious. We often only make surface-level judgments about what we assume we need and can predict. Without realizing that it's often the depth of that unnecessary thing that makes it interesting. And this depth hides gems of insight which contain immense meaning. Making that effort often feels unnecessary and designing on autopilot feels more controlled. What I am saying is that, sometimes, you **have to actually work to activate curiosity.**

Counterintuitivity · making meaningful innovation

"Make The Ordinary Unknown"

· Counterintuitivity Principle 2 ·

WHY DO SO many of us hold back? There are many reasons. People may be egocentric—eager to impress others with their own thoughts, stories, and ideas. Perhaps they are apathetic—they don't care enough to ask, or they anticipate being bored by the answers they'd hear. They may be overconfident in their own knowledge and think they already know the answers. Or perhaps they worry that they'll ask the wrong question and be viewed as rude or incompetent. Regardless of the emotion that underwrites it, it appears to me that most people—even those active in innovation—just don't understand how beneficial curiosity can be. If they did, they would end far fewer sentences with a period—and a lot more with a question mark.

Bang & Olufsen[65], the Danish manufacturer of music players and speakers, illustrates what happens when a brand works with more 'full stops' and not enough 'question marks.' Its people have believed that its success depended on achieving the ultimate pureness of sound, creating beautiful objects, delighting users through great physical product interfaces, and thinking of music as an in-home ex-

15 The nine principles of Counterintuitivity

perience. As a result, it has viewed architects and industrial designers as the best interpreters of customers' aspirations. And they used the pinnacle of sound technology to back up their stance and belief that only B&O can deliver a luxury in-home auditory experience. They did not question anything else and dismissed that which did not underscore their pursuit of high-end quality. That impeded the brand from reacting to the sudden rise of MP3 digital encoding. It's this music format that changed the world of music, making it more accessible, shareable, and portable.

However, the people at B&O saw the MP3 format as a lower quality of sound, and that this would not be of interest for the brand's reputation and belief system. Their mode of operating was to provide beautiful speakers and audio equipment, and the consumption of MP3 was largely on cheap, low-quality headphones or on the low-end built-in speaker of a computer. By not questioning the ordinary any deeper than their own bias allowed them, B&O missed the fact that it was the digital sphere that consumers saw as more meaningful than the physicality of an object, and that listening on-the-go offered new possibilities, compared to a static at-home one. Synonymous with high-end quality sound, the brand missed the opportunity that this "outlandishly inferior"[66] new technology could bring them. Its people never moved position and wrote off MP3 as something people "had" to use, not recognizing that it was what people wanted to use.

Today the brand is still on the outskirts of the digital offer, so much so that it wasn't until mid-2018 that it launched its own e-commerce website, beostore.com.

---

[65] https://www.bang-olufsen.com/ent
[66] http://productionadvice.co.uk/why-mp3-sounds-bad/

"THE IMPORTANT THING IS NOT TO STOP QUESTIONING. CURIOSITY HAS ITS OWN REASON OF EXISTING."

Albert Einstein — theoretical physicist

For us-adults, curiosity is the hardest button to button. Too many of us have forgotten how to access it and use it as fertile soil for ideas and possibilities. We mistake our sense of curiosity for the learned shame of not knowing or understanding. But as we all know, it is the spark that can lead to breakthrough innovation. And yet, while we may say we value inquisitiveness, too often, we stifle it. Because it is faster and a lot more efficient to think of what we 'know.' Knowledge feels like comfortable warm waters. But it is the trap door to mediocrity.

Knowledge blocks curiosity from happening. Not knowing is a strength rather than a weakness. It allows us to be open to new ideas, different opinions, to a world we may never have otherwise known. Being human, we tend to build an internal world where we feel very confident about how things are. We like to know; it gives a sense of security, even a sense of power. But as we start to look at what our mind starts to create from it, we see it often sets a very fixed way of thinking. A fixed way of thinking leads to a fixed way of doing, a fixed way of relating to others. A fixed way of thinking has people hold on to a fixed opinion, often only looking for those who support it, while keeping away or ignoring those whose opinions do not match. To a child everything is relevant; little is unseen. Once you look at what seems ordinary long enough, it often turns odd and unfamiliar, as any child repeatedly saying his own name aloud learns.

15 The nine principles of Counterintuitivity

Most of the breakthrough discoveries and remarkable inventions throughout history, from flints for starting a fire to self-driving cars, have something in common: They are the result of curiosity. The impulse to seek new information and experiences and explore novel possibilities is a basic human attribute. When our curiosity is triggered, we think more deeply and rationally about decisions and come up with more creative solutions. In addition, curiosity allows leaders to gain more respect from their followers and inspires employees to develop more trusting and more collaborative relationships with colleagues. So I encourage you to ask questions. Our future may depend on it.

It ain't what you don't know that gets you into trouble, it's what you know for sure that just ain't so. If you've seen the movie, The Big Short—and you should, it's great—you'll know that the movie opens with this quote, and credits it to Mark Twain. It's a perfect quote for the film, only it does not appear in any of Twain's books, essays, letters, or speeches. Because Mark Twain never wrote it or said it or anything like it. The closest he came is "Faith is believing what you know ain't so," which appears in Pudd'nhead Wilson's New Calendar and is a long way away from the quote that opens the movie. In fact, as far as I can tell, no one ever went on record and said that exact quote. Interestingly, Michael Lewis's book, The Big Short opens with this similar quote from Leo Tolstoy:

"*The most difficult subjects can be explained to the most slow-witted man if he has not formed any idea of them already; but the simplest thing cannot be made clear to the most intelligent man if he is firmly persuaded that he knows already, without a shadow of a doubt, what is laid before him.*"

Can we accept that, in truth, we really don't know? Sure, we will have a thought, an idea, an opinion. We may even have a belief. That is all imperfectly fine, it's human of us. But can we accept that we don't know? Can we look at the ordinary—either the familiar or the unworthy—and embrace that it is in the "not knowing" of that ordinary where we find real insight, true meaning, actual strength, and new possibilities? We find discovery and ultimately contentment. A sense of relaxation and calm others identify as confidence and knowledge. However, it does not come from knowledge, but from the detachment of that what we know. Now, it takes a certain amount of courage to let go of that old thinking, to let go of that stance of 'knowing.' When we do, minds are much more open, tolerance is much more present, and as a result, relationships with those around us change fundamentally. New ideas are emerging, decision making is improved because we have raised our susceptibility to stereotypes and confirmation bias.

Reality still leaves much to the imagination. If we care to look beyond what we see as known and ordinary. As an enabler of creativity, and a pursuer of innovation, your role is to nourish and nurture your own curiosity and evoke it in others. **Curiosity is creativity made visible.**

15 The nine principles of Counterintuitivity

Counterintuitivity · making meaningful innovation

"Choose More Boredom"

· *Counterintuitivity Principle 3* ·

CHANCES ARE THAT you're doing something else while you're reading this book. You might be in a meeting, working on a proposal, talking or texting to someone on the phone, listen to music, working out in the gym, having dinner, or keeping your Facebook page refreshed.

Am I right? Even if you're 100% concentrated on reading this page, you probably regularly engage in some multitasking throughout your day. Most of us do. We think it's a good thing to be busy. But if your answer to "how are you?" is "Busy", I regret to break it to you but you don't have a life. You may identify being busy with being successful, and that a full calendar means you are doing something right and important. But the truth is if all you are is busy, you don't have control over your own life. That is not a very meaningful way to go about the day, is it?

When did we all get so obsessed with productivity? We likely all experienced pressures about getting more work done. Software companies say their have the tools to help you work faster. We go to workshops and seminars to increase our efficiency. But is relentlessly pursuing productivity actually good for innovation? And is it really how we want to work? Despite our obsession with moving

15 The nine principles of Counterintuitivity

faster and doing more, productivity growth rates have stalled significantly in the last decade. According to the Bureau of Labor Statistics[67], we're only getting about 1.4% more productive per year, the lowest growth rate in 30 years. We're producing more productivity tools than ever, but we have less and less to show for it.

Perhaps even more problematic, it turns out a "do more, faster" mindset isn't actually how people want to work in the first place. In a survey of American knowledge workers[68], 61% say they want to "slow down to get things right," while only 41% say they want to "go fast to achieve more." So why are so many companies so focused on increasing productivity at all costs? Even when they set out to innovate, and test new ideas and unproven solutions, it is often done within the boundaries of efficiency.

I believe the issue here is precedent. Traditional industries like manufacturing have concrete ways to measure efficiency. If you can produce more goods over time with fewer resources, you've increased your productivity, and with it profitability. It's a mindset that dates back to the Industrial Revolution, and it remains a fixture for many modern-day businesses.

But the productivity calculus is much murkier when it comes to knowledge work—work that mostly involves dealing with new information, data and technology. Innovation work. Indeed, the Bureau of Labor Statistics cautions that productivity stats "for non-manufacturing industries are often difficult to measure" and that "customers should be cautious when interpreting the data." Do more lines of code per hour lead to better products? Would doubling the number of brainstorms per week make designers more creative?

---

[67] https://www.bls.gov/opub/btn/volume-6/below-trend-the-us-productivity-slowdown-since-the-great-recession.htm
[68] https://www.bls.gov/mfp/mprdload.htm

Even in the face of inconclusive data, the desire to do more with less persists—particularly among upper management. At many companies, a decision maker or manager picks the team's tools and sets the working cadence. But for those doing the work, these tools and timelines can create more problems than opportunities. In its 2018 Human Capital Trends report[69], Deloitte found that 47% of business and HR leaders were concerned that modern collaboration tools weren't actually helping businesses achieve their goals. Between chat windows, project management tools, meeting alerts, and emails, workers find themselves in a constant state of reactive busyness—rather than proactively focusing on meaningful work.

"GOOD PERSONS WILL NOT WASTE THEMSELVES BY BEING BUSY MERELY FOR THE SAKE OF BEING BUSY."

Seneca — Ancient Roman statesman, stoic philosopher

Our industry has been really good at finding ways to make the treadmill go faster. We're hiring people for their minds, and then we're not giving them any space to think. Being perpetually busy has one major downside that directly impacts our ability to achieve anything of great significance. It inhibits our ability to get into a flow. Significant accomplishments and flow are birds of a feather. We are in a habit to be working on the next thing while we're doing the current thing at the same time. We think that being busy is a badge of honor. In a world of constant connection and competition, many of us have adopted the habit of loading ourselves up with tasks. This addiction to busyness is causing us to go through our

---

[69] https://www2.deloitte.com/global/en/pages/human-capital/topics/future-of-work.html

15 The nine principles of Counterintuitivity

days on auto-pilot. Extending to the way we handle our personal and family lives.

That may ring true for many of us—but so what if it does? This is the twenty-first century, we're career-oriented, and we like to stay connected with friends on social media. Isn't it better to be busy than just sitting around doing nothing? We may think being constantly busy without pause, and that constantly being "on" is a good thing. But it is not. Being "on" at all times raises our cortisol levels, putting us in a near-constant state of stress[70]. We're addicted to the doing. Something many of us have grown used to, or are experiencing as being expected to live with. To counter this chronic stress at the workplace, the counterintuitive principle I want to introduce to our practice is 'boredom'.

Ages ago, when people were busy trying to survive, boredom wasn't a choice. They spent all their time securing food or shelter; they didn't have time to get bored. In contrast, today we overstimulate ourselves. We're always busy and feel the need to be. Once we recognise we are busy, we crave for more time, because we never seem to have enough. However, when we have free time, we don't know what to do with it. Nothing seems exciting enough to deserve our valuable time. So we best spend it being busy. When we do end up doing nothing, we get bored. But that is not always such a bad thing.

As Dr. Sandi Mann, the author of The Upside of Downtime: Why Boredom is Good[71], explains: "The more entertained we are, the more entertainment we need to feel satisfied. The more we fill our world with fast-moving, high-intensity, ever-changing stimulation,

---
[70] https://www.apa.org/news/press/releases/stress/2015/snapshot
[71] https://www.bookdepository.com/Upside-Downtime-Dr-Sandi-Mann/9781472135995

the more we get used to that and the less tolerant we become of lower levels." And soon we accept the false truth that being busy is better than being idle. That rational runs our professions, demanding that we utilise every minute of every working hour for the approval of our employer and our colleagues. Most of us would shudder at the thought of being caught "doing nothing."

And so it is that the second most commonly suppressed emotion in the workplace, runner up to anger, is boredom. We avoid it because we think we have a duty to be busy. We change jobs, careers and roles because of a perceived sense of boredom. It's interesting how boredom gets such a bad rap. We are quick to write off boredom as a pointless waste of time. However, that uneasy, awful feeling of boredom makes people keen to engage in activities they find more meaningful than those they are doing.

Boredom is not a negative, pointless emotion. It is a gateway to meaning. Foremost, it is a sanitizer. Imagine being perpetually excited by everything and everyone, every time and all the time. How exhausting! It may be counterintuitive to state, but I feel we can all do with more boredom in our working lives. Boredom has people think more creatively than those who are not allowing themselves to experience it.

Boredom is when we're searching for something to stimulate us we can't find in our immediate surroundings. We find that stimulation by letting our minds wander and go in different places in our heads. That kick-starts creativity, because once you daydream and allow your mind to wander, you think beyond the conscious and into the subconscious. This process allows your creativity to consider different and unexpected connections. Boredom offers the human mind more potential to consider new possibilities. Busy minds

15 The nine principles of Counterintuitivity

do not, and only enforce known patterns. The art is in not resisting the perceived distracting thoughts.

When we are consciously doing things—when we are busy—we're using our *"executive attention network."* The parts of the brain that control and police our attention. As neuroscientist Marcus Raichle[72] put it, "The attention network makes it possible for us to relate directly to the world around us, i.e., the here and now." When our minds wander, we activate a different part of our brain which Dr. Raichle calls the *"default mode network."* This default mode is our brain "at rest"; when we're not focused on an external, goal-oriented task. So, contrary to the popular view, when we space out, our mind isn't switched off. It is being primed to be innovative.

When we lose focus on the outside world and drift inward, we're not shutting down. When we bring our mind to "rest" we bring our creative energy inside-out. We're tapping into a vast trove of memories, imagining future possibilities, dissecting our interactions with other people, and reflecting on who we are. We label this as wasting precious time, but the brain is putting ideas into perspective. That makes daydreaming different from other forms of cognition. Rather than experiencing, organizing, and understanding things based on how they come to us from the outside world, we do it from within our own internal cognitive system. From our own unique perspective and meaning-making.

That allows for reflection and the ability for greater understanding. Being chronically busy and rushed for time impedes contemplation. Forcing this when our minds are on executive attention time sees our effort unrewarded. Ironically, it heightens the sense of busyness and the notion we are short on time. But in the shower

---

[72] https://en.wikipedia.org/wiki/Marcus_Raichle

or on a drive the next day, when your brain relives the moment, your thoughts become more nuanced. You not only think of a million possibilities, you get a different perspective and gain insights. This applies not only to ideation, but even in tension and arguments. Reflecting about a personal interaction, rather than reacting the way you did when you encountered it in the real world, is a profound form of creativity spurred on by allowing the mind to first wander in the default mode. The secret to listening lives here; when your mind is free of agenda, argument or the need to debate.

The habit to create and imagine is to move from boredom to mind wandering. We need to prompt our mind to wander, as counterintuitive as that may feel. If we don't wander, boredom bring us to 'being bored'. When boredom leads to being bored, we choose escapism. We avoid self-reflection and disconnect from our environment, and everything it can offer us. So my point isn't to have us stop doing and take long breaks of nothing-ness. My proposal is to balance action with reflection. Doing with wandering. If we insert more reflection habits into our working day, our time at work becomes much more meaningful and positive. Because if we don't, and all we do is sit there submerged in busyness, we end up doing more of what we find meaningless.

At first thought, boredom and brilliance are completely at odds with each other. They are, however, inner related. Boredom, if defined just as the state of being weary and restless through lack of interest, does has negative connotations and is to be avoided at all costs. Boredom when seen through the light of allowing new stimulus to inspire different thinking is something to aspire to—a quality of innovative mental ability. It's not immediately clear for most of us, but these two opposing states are in fact intimately connected. You could say that boredom is an incubator for brilliance to manifest

15 The nine principles of Counterintuitivity

itself. It's the messy, uncomfortable, confusing, frustrating place one has to occupy for a while before finally coming up with the winning idea or enticing possibility. When you allow your mind to rest and **accept boredom's invitation** to have your mind wander and reflect, your senses become heightened, and you notice things you wouldn't have otherwise.

You might feel uncomfortable, annoyed, or even angry at first, but who knows what you can accomplish once you get through the first phases of boredom and trigger some of its amazing side effects.

Counterintuitivity · making meaningful innovation

"Create Moments of Affinity"

· *Counterintuitivity Principle 4* ·

SIXTEEN THOUSAND—THAT'S HOW many words we speak, on average, each day. Imagine how many unspoken ones course through your mind and extend that to the minds of those around you. Most of our thoughts are not facts but evaluations and judgments entwined with emotions—some positive and helpful, others negative and less so. The prevailing wisdom says that difficult thoughts and feelings have no place at the office: Executives, and particularly leaders, should be either stoic or cheerful; they must project confidence and damp down any negativity bubbling up inside them. But that goes against basic biology. All healthy human beings have an inner stream of thoughts and feelings that include criticism, doubt, and fear. That's just our minds doing the job they were designed to do: trying to anticipate and solve problems and avoid potential pitfalls.

However, if every member of a team doesn't commit to growing together, they will grow apart. Various studies show that how we feel about the work we do very much depends on the relationships with our coworkers and clients. And what are relationships other than a string of micro-interactions? There are dozens of these every day, each one has the potential to be meaningful. When how we

---

[73] https://www.gallup.com/workplace/229424/employee-engagement.aspx

15 The nine principles of Counterintuitivity

interact and relate to each other is of meaning to us, we design and develop more of what could be meaningful to others.

A survey by Gallup, an American management consulting company founded by George Gallup in 1935, known for its public opinion polls, said that 27% of bosses believe their employees are inspired and engaged by their colleagues. However, in the same survey, only four percent of employees agreed with that statement. If your workforce is typical, about one-third of your employees or colleagues are actively engaged. The poll found that nearly half, or 49%, are disengaged while 18% are actively disengaged. The biggest concern with this is the potential loss of an organization's most valued talent. The numbers might be better when we just look within the creative industry, but it does make you wonder; if these are the clients we work with and for—what are our chances of designing more meaningfully? If, as a driver of meaningful innovation, improving engagement has not been on your radar screen, it now should be. Gallup's research[73] is a meta-analysis across 199 studies covering 152 organizations, 44 industries, and 26 countries. It showed that high employee engagement brings an uplift of every business performance number. Profitability up 16%, productivity up 18%, customer loyalty up 12% and quality up an incredible 60%. We know that life is not just about efficiency. So why do we resist the idea that work can be about greatness?

"TRUE JOY RESULTS WHEN WE BECOME AWARE OF OUR CONNECTEDNESS TO EVERYTHING."

Dr. Paul Pearsall — lecturer, author

Counterintuitivity · making meaningful innovation

The secret of a healthy relationship is not the great gesture or the lofty promise, it's small moments of affinity. Creating these is a wonderful design challenge.

Today, design and innovation leaders are faced with a need to facilitate collaborations creatively different. I believe that when leading creatively by creating small moments of affinity, what we do is connect with others through improbable connections. And evoke something that might be—yes—unpredictable, and also—yes—seemingly unnecessary. But instead of a manipulated loyalty, we playfully create attachment at will.

Our agency was engaged to offer consult to a major financial institution. Several meetings were required, and I found myself feeling anxious, dismissive, and judgmental toward one of the project leaders there. This was based on my interactions with him and on what others had said of theirs. The experiences of us working with him gave me a rather closed and rigid impression of him. In my eyes, his responses held insulting behavior and whatever I would say would be met with an arrogant comment from him. But our defences were unwarranted and our assumption that he was a jerk proved wrong. He was engaging, open to learning, and willing to accept his need to improve. His fear was to be so harsh toward others that he would exclude and alienate himself, and he seemed stumped and genuinely troubled by how we had come to characterize him as such. What our relationship lacked was affinity and attachment, and it was not until we had reached a breaking point, that all of us realized it.

When I ran my own design studio, SGTH, I created a seemingly random and irrelevant tradition called "Freaky Friday." Once or twice a quarter, at different Fridays and a day's notice, I asked all of us to wear a mask during office hours. To be worn all day; at

15 The nine principles of Counterintuitivity

the desks, over lunch, during important meetings, even with our biggest clients, who were invited—leveraging a good dose of peer pressure—to join in. Almost always, they would. On Freaky Fridays, we'd all leave the studio with aligned outcomes and full of enthusiasm. Eager for Mondays to get back to it.

What I am saying is **never to underestimate the power of a ridiculous mask**. Obviously, I am not advocating you to do this exact thing. But here's what I learned: Hierarchy kills affinity and masks erase hierarchy. Masks allow us to use the disguise of the false to show something true about ourselves. Showing something true about yourself creates moments of affinity. It creates attachment, even meaning, between people. People you work with or for. Affinity, and the humanness that it brings, increases the quality and potential of an innovation. Because you perform your job in reflection of the affinity you have with those people that join you on that journey. It's pure emotion: attachment-at-will instead of manipulated loyalty. Keeping play and joy at the heart of what we do, enhancing our willingness and openness to participation, and collaboratively building on ideas, creativity, and possibilities. Creating moments of affinity makes innovation efforts meaningful again.

But it's not easy in our everyday work lives, because the relationship with our colleagues or with our clients may have grown apart, suffered betrayals and disappointments, and are now in need to be meaningful for one another once again. And for any of us, the first step toward being meaningful involves a risk. The risk to be a little ugly. **To be imperfect.**

"Dare To Be A Little Ugly"

· *Counterintuitivity Principle 5* ·

AUTHENTICITY IS GAINING traction in the field of leadership, but what does it mean to be authentic? Authenticity is about the congruence between our deeper values and beliefs and our actions. An authentic person puts the people around them at ease, like a comforting, old friend who welcomes us in and makes us feel at home. When there is a lack of congruence, this leads to an emotional force that seeks reduction. Although many of us would agree with the folk wisdom that we should try to be ourselves, social-cognitive theories have no way of making sense of this statement.

Today, being authentic is mostly understood as showing off your beautiful side, and labeling it 'your true self.' However, I would argue that being authentic means daring to show your ugly side. There is an irony in being authentic in the age of algorithms. We know that authenticity is a differentiator from the artificial. And so, we have started to prescribe how authenticity can be expressed in repeatable patterns, with consistency and standardization. This kind of authenticity can already be found on social media where it offers a visual sea of mimicry, and as such, it reverses the actual context of being authentic. @Insta_repeat[74] posts collages made up of photos by unrelated photographers that look remarkably similar. The account put into question the authenticity of the travel blogs and accounts they are poached from while shining a light on the power of visual

15 The nine principles of Counterintuitivity

lessly exploring and questioning their surroundings—every time, all the time. They will venture out and crawl anywhere; down a flight of stairs, through an open window, into a swimming pool. They will put their hands in the mouth of a dog, grab knives or forks, put their fingers into electric sockets, reach for a cup of hot coffee. They do all that because they don't know any other fear besides the two mentioned. We are each of us born practically free of fears, only to become fearful as we grow up.

All the fear you have today you have acquired. They have been instructed to us, we have been conditioned for them. When you hear others—or perhaps yourself—say 'I am scared of being rejected,' or 'I don't want to speak out of terms,' or even 'I don't like it when people look at me, or ask me questions' these are all fears that we acquired. It paralyzes perfectly functioning humans from being the person they naturally are.

But, as humans, we are naturally fearless. Each of us, as a toddler, was constantly being looked at by dozens of people. Our parents, family, perhaps siblings. Doctors, nurses, caregivers. Friends, neighbors and acquaintances. Some would playfully grab your chubby leg and count your tiny toes. No baby or toddler will resist this attention, or shy away thinking 'don't look at me, I am not good enough, I don't belong here.' 'I don't have anything smart to say'; toddlers don't have any of these concerns. Babies and toddlers love attention, love to participate and feel included. They may have their diaper at full capacity, it won't hold them back in interacting naturally and out of affinity and curiosity.

Counterintuitivity · making meaningful innovation

"DON'T LET THE FEAR OF WHAT COULD HAPPEN HAVE NOTHING HAPPEN."

Doe Zantamata — Author

The fear of being judged is an acquired fear, it is a learned fear. We learn to fear being judged because we all have likely experienced being judged unkindly or unfavorably. We've been compared, evaluated, and rated against standards and requirements. We've fallen short of established or perceived expectations. The taste is bitter, the sting nasty. You can overcome all that by judging yourself internally with kindness and positivity. The judgment we fear is the external one; our mind narrates scenarios like 'What if I ask this, and the other person looks at me as if I am stupid?' 'What if I say this, and they call me out on it, and I have to explain it again?' or 'I better not question that or I will annoy him or her.' External fears; disappointment, rejection, hurt, pain. It's okay to go through all of these, it is okay that these fears always seem to come back. You're at your learning edge when they do. It's an offer to grow, shape, and mold yourself further—fear is a learning experience.

That innate, internal, fear of falling we all have? It is that plummeting feeling in your stomach when you stand at height, looking down. You feel that when the attention of a room shifts to you as you speak. When you stand in front of an audience, whether it is your team or client, or at an event or conference. Now, this fear is more palpable. We feel our hands are colder, perhaps with a little tremble, and we can't tell if this is nerves or excitement. Because it is both. This inner nervousness is our defense mechanism against falling—not failing. If we register this as a fear of failing, we interpret this as a signal that the situation does not deserve; the natural instinct to

15 The nine principles of Counterintuitivity

trends and their sources. With the worldwide Instagram influencer market value projected to reach 2.38 billion US dollars in 2019, and our feeds dictated by an algorithm that favors 'relevant' content, superficiality is now an all-you-can-eat buffet that, with the advent of smartphone camera technology, is just so easy to replicate. And so we do, we share the self we think we need to be, not the life we actually have. Our flaws, mistakes, imperfections are disappearing from view, leaving a warped reality of what is deemed human. Authenticity is being re-contextualized.

Mid-2012, we were asked to hold an intervention to transform a brand reversing its struggling business. On the outside looking in, this was a beautiful-looking company. Their products looked great and customers expressed their appreciation, their people were talented and seen within their industry as leaders and specialists. And their office looked like one of those urban hipster resorts slash coffee temples. The kind of place that looked attractive and would make the brand a desirable employer. Once inside, however, we were struck by the notion that they were uncomfortable in their own skins. So, as part of the process, we jointly identified, named, and pinned on large boards all the issues—and there were several dozen of them—that had all become obstacles to better performance. We put them on boards, moved the boards into the conference room, which we renamed "the ugly room." The ugly became visible for everyone to see—staff, management, visitors, partners, suppliers. The ugly was celebrated. The ugly room served as a mirror and as a social learning space. **Celebrate your ugly room**, these are your obstacles to better performance.

---

[74] https://www.instagram.com/insta_repeat/

Counterintuitivity · making meaningful innovation

"WE ARE CONSTANTLY INVITED TO BE WHO WE ARE."

Henry David Thoreau — Essayist, poet, philosopher.

To be authentic, we must allow ourselves to be imperfect. If leaders want to unleash individual and collective talent, they must foster a psychologically safe climate where employees feel free, and true to their true selves, to contribute ideas, share information, and report mistakes. The good, the bad, and the ugly. Authentic workplaces don't try to make everyone the same.

Bill George[75], the former CEO of Medtronic, often speaks of climbing the corporate ladder early in his career at Honeywell and becoming disillusioned with himself. He mentions wearing cufflinks to try to impress the board of directors. He recalls, "One day I'm driving home. It's a beautiful day. I looked in the mirror, and I'm miserable. I don't like the businesses I'm in. I'm not passionate about that but most importantly, I don't like myself." George was acting inauthentically to impress others and had a personal transformation which led him to switch industries and begin acting in a way that felt more congruent with his "true self." Notably, in George's retelling of the transformation, it was sparked by looking in a mirror which presumably heightens one's consciousness of the self. He had built and recognized his "ugly room." George would eventually move on to Medtronic and write several books about authentic leadership. He would also help develop the course "Authentic Leadership,"[76] which is a central course on leadership at Harvard Business School. Wanting and matching the predictable patterns of what is hailed as authentic, yes: it can be presented as being beautiful. To

---

[75] https://www.billgeorge.org/
[76] https://www.exed.hbs.edu/authentic-leader-development/

15 The nine principles of Counterintuitivity

be authentic is to be a little ugly. It's not adhering to a pattern, it's adhering to who you are, regardless of the pattern.

So many of us are afraid to try being authentic because we are thinking about the ridicule or questioning we may receive from being our own selves, in public, on purpose, all the time. But you have to be comfortable in the skin that you're in. Because by you being comfortable in yours, you will allow someone else to be comfortable in theirs. Another—priceless—moment of affinity.

Allow and celebrate your little uglinesses, your rough edges, your imperfections. It's what makes you "you"—it's what makes you **unpredictably human.**

Counterintuitivity · making meaningful innovation

"Forget How To Fear"

· *Counterintuitivity Principle 6* ·

THE MOST REGRETFUL people on earth are those who felt the call to create or contribute, who felt their own creative power restive and uprising, and gave to it neither power nor time. There is something lovely about this notion of giving time—a generous counterpoint to our culture of taking time, snatching it from the river of being with the fist of disciplined demand, only to see it slip through. The discipline of showing up is an absolutely necessary condition for all creative work, yes, but it is not a sufficient one. Sometimes—often—we show up, only to find nothing happens. Whatever it is we are showing up for cannot be willed. We learn then that the work is the work, but the work is also the waiting—the exasperation, the surrender to despair, and the swell of joy on the other side of the surrender. On the other side of fear. Fear that often asks us larger, unanswerable questions about the measure of a good idea all the way to what it means to leave a lasting mark of betterment on an imperfect world. What meaningful proposals have gone unspoken because those who imagined them could not overcome their fear of speaking them?

Fear. That debilitating shackle, holding us back, unhinging us from being us. To think that we are born with only two true fears; human babies and toddlers have a fear of being dropped, and a fear of loud noises. That's it. Nothing else is feared. Toddlers will be fear-

15 The nine principles of Counterintuitivity

lessly exploring and questioning their surroundings—every time, all the time. They will venture out and crawl anywhere; down a flight of stairs, through an open window, into a swimming pool. They will put their hands in the mouth of a dog, grab knives or forks, put their fingers into electric sockets, reach for a cup of hot coffee. They do all that because they don't know any other fear besides the two mentioned. We are each of us born practically free of fears, only to become fearful as we grow up.

All the fear you have today you have acquired. They have been instructed to us, we have been conditioned for them. When you hear others—or perhaps yourself—say 'I am scared of being rejected,' or 'I don't want to speak out of terms,' or even 'I don't like it when people look at me, or ask me questions' these are all fears that we acquired. It paralyzes perfectly functioning humans from being the person they naturally are.

But, as humans, we are naturally fearless. Each of us, as a toddler, was constantly being looked at by dozens of people. Our parents, family, perhaps siblings. Doctors, nurses, caregivers. Friends, neighbors and acquaintances. Some would playfully grab your chubby leg and count your tiny toes. No baby or toddler will resist this attention, or shy away thinking 'don't look at me, I am not good enough, I don't belong here.' 'I don't have anything smart to say'; toddlers don't have any of these concerns. Babies and toddlers love attention, love to participate and feel included. They may have their diaper at full capacity, it won't hold them back in interacting naturally and out of affinity and curiosity.

Counterintuitivity · making meaningful innovation

"DON'T LET THE FEAR OF WHAT COULD HAPPEN HAVE NOTHING HAPPEN."

Doe Zantamata — Author

The fear of being judged is an acquired fear, it is a learned fear. We learn to fear being judged because we all have likely experienced being judged unkindly or unfavorably. We've been compared, evaluated, and rated against standards and requirements. We've fallen short of established or perceived expectations. The taste is bitter, the sting nasty. You can overcome all that by judging yourself internally with kindness and positivity. The judgment we fear is the external one; our mind narrates scenarios like 'What if I ask this, and the other person looks at me as if I am stupid?' 'What if I say this, and they call me out on it, and I have to explain it again?' or 'I better not question that or I will annoy him or her.' External fears; disappointment, rejection, hurt, pain. It's okay to go through all of these, it is okay that these fears always seem to come back. You're at your learning edge when they do. It's an offer to grow, shape, and mold yourself further—fear is a learning experience.

That innate, internal, fear of falling we all have? It is that plummeting feeling in your stomach when you stand at height, looking down. You feel that when the attention of a room shifts to you as you speak. When you stand in front of an audience, whether it is your team or client, or at an event or conference. Now, this fear is more palpable. We feel our hands are colder, perhaps with a little tremble, and we can't tell if this is nerves or excitement. Because it is both. This inner nervousness is our defense mechanism against falling—not failing. If we register this as a fear of failing, we interpret this as a signal that the situation does not deserve; the natural instinct to

15 The nine principles of Counterintuitivity

prevent falling is said to date back from when we lived as primates in trees or on steep mountain slopes to stay out of reach of predators. If these signals, however, are not managed properly, we acquire a learned external fear. Such as the fear of public speaking, the fear of expressing a thought or idea.

We fill ourselves up with fear. What if I speak and get laughed at? What if I try that and it doesn't work? What if I am told I am wrong? Why would my idea work in the first place? What does it say of me if I cannot see anything in this research? How will they trust me if I don't understand anything from their industry or profession? All scenarios running in your mind that explore 'what could go wrong.' What is the worst possible outcome here? There is honestly no point in these fears. When you focus and devote attention to the worst possible outcome, that imaginary story in your mind—you live and experience as if you already are in that scenario. Your senses, emotions and thought patterns are skewed toward it. You create the lens through which you will find the evidence of that fear. It will be debilitating.

Evaluations like 'falling short of' or 'falling flat' are but designed constructs that serve to fill ourselves up with fear. But you don't have to feel that fear because every sense or trigger of fear is a teachable moment for yourself. To do more, to be more. Your talent as a designer or innovator is too valuable to be sabotaged by fear. The most immediate countermeasure against fearing the worst, is reversing the storyline to imagine the best possible outcome. 'There is this idea I have that I don't fully see as a solution, but maybe I can spark someone else's imagination with it.' It is a matter of changing your belief system. With fears being acquired, we have adopted a belief system. You can change those beliefs. Ideas, thoughts, and hunches are only guesses until they become actions. It is not enough to simply tell people your inner thoughts; you need to take those insights and put them into action to see where they might lead. To do so, you must act in order to understand. That's not scary; that's exciting and energizing! This willingness to reveal and share yourself in service of a larger goal is what makes a work of innovation meaningful and authentic.

Fear is a choice. **You can choose not to fear.** Research[77] states that our thinking improves by 31% when we are in a positive mood. Thirty-one percent—that is no small jump. Start by smiling, internally. Your designer and innovating mind are already primed for rational and inspirational storylines; you can talk yourself out of fear and overcome it by smiling internally at the prospect of delivering your idea. The next time fear wells up in you, you have a choice. Do you enable the worst or the best possible outcome?

---

[77] https://www.huffpost.com/entry/positive-thinking_n_3512202
https://www.ncbi.nlm.nih.gov/pmc/articles/PMC3156028/

15 The nine principles of Counterintuitivity

Counterintuitivity · making meaningful innovation

"Change Is Permanent"

· *Counterintuitivity Principle 7* ·

DAVID BOWIE'S SONG said it best: "Cha-Cha-Changes, turn and face the strange changes." Everything is changing, and it is weird when it does. Nothing ever stays the same. In that respect, the world and our lives on it are as they should be, but may again never be as they were. It is meant to be in a permanent state of change. There is great energy and freedom to be found in accepting this straightforward truth; change is always happening. Various things change at various speeds; evolutionary or by design. Cause and effect or initiated. Accidental or prescribed. Of course, often, the way we want to live our lives, run our careers, our businesses and our relationships, is to resist that straightforward truth that everything is meant to change. We may outwardly signal that we like the idea of change, inwardly, our minds have created this story in which we have constructed the right emotions to make us feel nice and secure when there is not too much change, or no risk of change happening.

Most of us like the idea of a little bit of change, break a routine of sorts, a trip somewhere. As long as that change doesn't happen too much, and not too frequently. As long as we have a fair degree of certainty about what change is going to bring. Because of that narrative, we have collectively imagined the state of no-change, or as-little-change-as-possible, to be a safe place. But is it, though? This imagined safe place holds us back from meaningfully experiencing

15 The nine principles of Counterintuitivity

the fullness of life, along with the potential of its possibilities. When we live, think and act from within, that idea that only a little change is okay, all we really aim for is predictability. We walk the narrow path of iteration. Now, imagine what could change if we let go of that idea, and allow thoughts that recognize everything is, and has to be, changing?

For me, doing this generates an energy. With that comes a sense of freedom, for both my mind and for my life. Allowing emotions to come and go. Allowing interactions around us to come and go. Even recognizing our own limitations and reservations as part of what is resisting change.

"PEOPLE ARE VERY OPEN-MINDED ABOUT NEW THINGS, SO LONG AS THEY ARE EXACTLY LIKE THE OLD ONES."

Charles F. Kettering — American inventor, engineer, businessman

You may ask yourself, who is crazy enough to resist innovation? And the true answer is: all of us. Because while the result of innovation can be excellent new products and services, the implementation of innovation brings about the dreaded C-word. Change. And believe me, any person, team, or corporation is completely capable of resisting change. One reason innovation is difficult to do is the undeniable fact that innovation introduces change. Innovation processes involve a multitude of changes that can affect anyone in the company that activates these. Changes in the way of establishing relationships between the various stakeholders in the company. Chang-

Counterintuitivity · making meaningful innovation

ing the tools used to develop the work. Changes in the nature of the job. Changes in the hierarchy of workers. Innovation can change the importance of the tasks. A task was marginal before and now is a primary task. Employees who perform these tasks may change their professional category or hierarchy in the company. Emergence of new tasks. The introduction of new infrastructure and tools often include the emergence of new figures of employees for management and maintenance. These changes, because they can be very numerous, and in principle, unknown to the people at the company, can produce negative feelings of anxiety, fear, worry, hostility, intrigue, polarization, conflict or impatience with and among employees. Often, these feelings can have two origins. Origin conscious, if feelings result from employee thinking, and origin unconscious, if feelings are the product of the influence of peers and not self-motivated. Regardless, it causes the same side effects: employees try to block change, they try to avoid changing their current situation and their working conditions.

To navigate this, I've conducted several working sessions—impromptu—using the resistance levels that employees have known to help them understand their empathy with the innovation process; from no resistance to distrust, to no collaboration offered, to hostility, to enemy. That sounds daunting, but I have actually never encountered anyone declaring themselves an enemy of innovation. Because people do identify themselves as hostile to it. You have someone who does not believe in innovation and also attempts to influence other workers of his or her belief. When they are not willing to accept innovation ideas and not wanting to participate in the process, they elect not to collaborate. Both these groups either need intervention to bring them along, or see them not partake in the effort. I usually find the majority of people that have a first encounter with innovation will place themselves in the Distrust segment.

15 The nine principles of Counterintuitivity

Meaning that they are unwilling to process innovation, not opposed to it happening, but unwilling to provide resources or contributions. In general, this position is maintained in the early stages of the innovation process until it evolves into a position of greater strength or becomes non-resistant. This is a fluent variable; people can shift position during the process of innovation. Collaboration is a choice; those that offered no resistance yesterday could suddenly be the blockers you encounter today.

At risk of generalizing it; most resistance to change comes out of a fear of loss; loss of control, freedom, ownership, position, security, etc. Resistance occurs during the transition, a psychological process of acknowledging what is ending, navigating the uncertainty, then embracing what is possible in the new beginning. Strengthening support networks, anchoring one's purpose, increasing self-compassion, and actualizing strengths can all minimize resistance. Take a look at your team or organization and its subtle but powerful resistors to innovation. Does the resistance arise from dissatisfaction with the current state? Does the resistance arise from a lack of vision about the future state? For those that are ahead of the pack, dissatisfaction may be their stumbling blocks. But maybe they suffer a lack of executive vision. I find that most organizations suffer from a lack of 'first concrete steps'.

Learning to define and take those steps will help dramatically reduce innovation resistance. In other words, part of the design of innovation is requiring you to think about creating the environment necessary for innovation to be embraced, rather than resisted or feared. I recall a project where we were asked to come help make a digital transformation actionable by working onsite—that is a fancy way of saying my design colleagues and I worked at the client's office. We were embedded, alongside those who were fearful of the decisions and actions that we were going to be imposing on them. It was in this setting that I first experimented with the resistance scale. I also used a little gimmick that I saw on the internet; a change jar. I went to buy the largest mason jar I could find, cut a slit in the lid, and stuck a label on it that said, "If you don't like change, leave it here." I inserted a few coins of my own and visibly placed the jar right at the entry of our project room. With the side note that the content would be used for coffee or beers at the end of the project. We never quite filled that thing, but this little act of affinity helped remind us all that change happens. Because it is supposed to.

"The more things change, the more they stay the same." Written in January 1849, Alphonse Karr understood a fundamentally human character trait; turbulent changes do not affect reality on a deeper level other than to anchor us even more to the status quo. I find it is a truism, succinctly explaining many of innovation's polarities. Bringing about change is exposing our resistance to it, bringing into full view the limitations of what we can accept, demanding this change to be meaningful. The bigger the change, the bigger the need to have it be of purpose and meaning.

Change is alteration. It is something that takes place that keeps something from being identical. Identical meaning something is exactly as how it was, or how we thought it to be. Every day, new technologies and trends open new opportunities to succeed—or to fail. Both success and failure is a change to how it was before. Although the unknown possibilities that come with change can be frightening, surviving in this environment means learning to quickly adapt to and embrace change, rather than meeting it with resistance. Imagine what a tolerance for change can help create; what if our innovations change after we made them? Instead of depreciating when you get or use them, they would actually increase in value or usefulness.

15 The nine principles of Counterintuitivity

The closest examples I know of is the Nest thermostat or the Tesla car. Both, just as their customers, are changing constantly, and are only getting smarter.

Everything is changing. The way we look at things is changing. What we see once, and see again, is seen differently. The things we are looking at are also changing all the time. Everything is changing because it is harder to pinpoint whether something remains identical than whether it has changed. Ironically, the only thing that is harder to realize is changing is ourselves. We change our emotions, our moods, our bodies, our opinions and ideas, our sentences and expressions. We surprise ourselves with the thoughts we have, or the resistances we bring up, missing altogether the notion that we are doing what we are supposed to be doing; changing. Now that we know we do it all the time, we could perhaps do it more meaningfully.

Counterintuitivity · making meaningful innovation

"Decisions Just Are"

· *Counterintuitivity Principle 8* ·

WHAT MAKES A good decision? When I ask teams, clients, or peers that question, I often get answers like: "When the outcome is successful." Why is it that we, as an industry and as a society, romanticize outcomes? Only things and people that succeed are celebrated. Just look at all the articles and books that idolize successful people. And to a degree that's obvious. And it feels warranted to highlight accomplishments, sure. But it's also misleading. We tend to overlook cases that did not come with a successful outcome. And when we do look at failure, we are often quick to explain why things failed. In hindsight, we can all look at mistakes and say that it was imminent. But if we are thinking that preventing mistakes is that easy, why are we still make decisions that we regret?

Take the case of the Titanic. Looking back, we all know that the luxury liner that traveled from Southampton to New York made many costly mistakes. But here's the thing: No one wanted the Titanic disaster to happen. And no one predicted it... Until after the fact. Then we found plenty of evidence of the 'bad' decisions made. It is now well known that the Titanic didn't carry enough lifeboats. "What happens in case of an emergency and the ship is at capacity?" is something that someone surely asked, right? We don't know, we weren't there. Then the Titanic was tested for six hours and never with a full crew. After that, they loaded up the passengers and set

15 The nine principles of Counterintuitivity

sail toward New York. "Shouldn't we try this thing out a few more times before we bring passengers on board?" someone surely said. Maybe no one actually did. But I doubt that. They more likely decided not to.

It's easy to look at success and attribute it all to good decision making. But here's the thing—that statement is also true the other way around. Failure is not always explained by bad decision making. However, that's what most historians do. But like Dostoevsky said: in hindsight, failure is always obvious. The people who were responsible for the Titanic probably thought they were making the right decisions at the time. After the fact, they probably regretted many things. But I don't think good or bad decisions have anything to do with the outcome. Good decisions can lead to bad outcomes just as well. Sometimes even bad decisions can lead to good outcomes. No matter the sensors, data, AI or machine learning: you can't predict the future. So that's why I think it's pointless when people pretend they can teach you how to make "good" decisions. There's no such thing; there is the decision you make and go with. And hindsight will be its judge.

"EVERYTHING SEEMS STUPID WHEN IT FAILS."

Fyodor Dostoevsky — Novelist, journalist, and philosopher.

The way you look at how something works in the real world is called a mental model. It's your thinking framework about something. When we make decisions, we often don't think about our framework and as a result, immediately jump to a discussion about potential outcomes. That's an illogical method because you're not questioning your decision-making process. You're only looking at the outcome. Can we consider what specific thinking frameworks,

Counterintuitivity · making meaningful innovation

or mental models, we can or should use for that decision we want to make? Too often, we skip the process and jump right to deciding. Maybe that's due to a lack of time, resources, or knowledge—it doesn't matter. Whatever the reason is, it's really not an excuse to skip the decision-making process altogether. Because that's the only way to become a bad decision maker—regardless of the outcome. The good news is, you don't have to know everything about mental models—I certainly don't.

There are scaffolds to use to bring conversations for understanding, to conversations for choice, toward conversations for decisions. The art of crafting effective strategic conversations is a little-known, yet high-impact sub-field of learning experience design. I'm fortunate that I work with other leaders and professional designers who are well versed in this discipline. Though many designers or innovators would no doubt excel at it, given the opportunity to apply their skills to this context. Designing a strategic conversation is not to be confused with organizing a meeting. Most competent professionals know how to convene a well-organized meeting; far fewer can pull off an effective strategic conversation to arrive at a decision.

The construct of this starts with building understanding first. This is basically a diagnostic session. It is called for when your team doesn't know much about a particular issue or has multiple divergent views. Overall, the purpose is to try to get alignment around specific insights and gain shared understanding. The challenge, however, can be keeping it at the knowledge-sharing level. People often try to rush to decision-making, but it's generally a bad idea to go from initial insight to decision-making in the same session. Think of yourself as a scout, not a soldier. When armies make plans for battles, or the tactics needed for conflict resolution, they first send out scouts. Scouts are not there to fight; they are there to lis-

15 The nine principles of Counterintuitivity

ten, observe, report. Scouts bring back understanding. They do not decide or take any action. They build an understanding of the total picture. That information will help shape choices. Once the issue is well understood, but the resolution is not, a shaping-choices conversation is needed. In this conversation, participants discuss different options based on their shared understanding of the situation, and evaluate the pros and cons of each.

The key practices in this type of strategic conversation are to develop a manageable number of options—say, three to five—and to also treat the status quo as one of them. After all, by putting "do nothing" on the table as a specific option, you can remove its "default" power and treat it as just one of several possible choices. Once there is understanding and the choices are evaluated, it is time to make a decision. While some organizations like to pretend that big strategic decisions are made in executive-team or management-committee meetings, that's usually not the case. Rather, most big decisions are made by leading players "offline" and then ratified in formal meetings. Decisions are typically shaped much further upstream—which can be all the more reason to focus the bulk of your energy on designing powerful strategic conversations around building understanding and shaping choices.

It won't help ensure the outcome of the decision. We simply cannot predict the future, nor can we know all mental models that exist. But we can **improve our conversation strategies** to arrive at decisions we don't regret in hindsight.

Counterintuitivity · making meaningful innovation

"Remain Incomplete And Unfinished"

· *Counterintuitivity Principle 9* ·

ALGORITHM. UNLESS YOU live disconnected from the universe, you've probably heard or read this word that has changed the world and has more influence on your life than you think, or possibly, like. A life where connected sensors are in our build and biological environment, generating ever more quantities of data. Abstract patterns of both known and prescribed expectations. Our life in the 21st century is a tale of me, myself, and AI. Now that the internet is no longer one thing, but all things, do we innovators finally have the means to understand people better than they understand themselves? Are these algorithms humankind's new best friend?

As a concept, an algorithm is nothing more than a sequence of actions taken to achieve a specific goal. Every day you run an array of algorithms, from the time you wake up to the moment you go to sleep. And when you sleep, your body also performs various algorithms. The action of preparing a juice or getting ready to go to work in the morning are other examples of micro-algorithms. And, yes, that favorite app on your smartphone. That, too, is a set of algorithms. It has a place in our world, I am not arguing that. More often than not, we, as people tend to always do the same things.

15 The nine principles of Counterintuitivity

We call this a routine. Certain aspects of our lives will benefit from streamlining the routine in it. From making something usable, to frictionless, to anticipatory. Or offering predictability to eliminate surprise or cognitive load. If I transfer money from my account to another, for example, I want routine and the predictability that this is happening without friction or surprise. How dull would life be if everything was routine, anticipated, and known? Is a life without friction more meaningful?

"TO ERR IS HUMAN, TO FORGIVE IS DIVINE"

Alexander Pope — poet

In a time of pervasive automation, personalized but anonymous interactions, and an overall Amazon-ization of the online experience, mistakes can make a brand appear more human—and being human is increasingly a crucial differentiator when competitors emphasize efficiency and expediency at any cost.

Perhaps some of you are familiar with Fado[78], a traditional, melancholic Portuguese music. It is a musical genre that cannot be automated by machines. Why? Fado is a collection of minor mistakes and small imperfections made by the musicians. Because there are no drums, the rhythm is mostly dictated by the singer. Which, according to the principles of music, is somewhat of a bad idea. It makes the beat unsteady, the rhythm somewhat trembling, and a performance volatile. These imperfections give the music a distinctive aura of vulnerability and heartache. Fado is distinctively human in its unrepeatable imperfections. Its 'mistakes' and friction are what make it meaningful.

---

[78] https://en.wikipedia.org/wiki/Fado

Counterintuitivity · making meaningful innovation

Friction can be a good thing. The 'value' of Starbucks' grab-and-go pre-order app is that you can get your coffee without having to make eye-contact with staff. Where is the brand experience? The humanness of retail commerce? Conversely, Starbucks Reserve is now the most meaningful way of getting people into the brand. Currently, Starbucks has opened one in New York and three other Reserve Roasteries in Seattle, Shanghai, and Milan. In 2019, new ones are planned for Tokyo (opening in late February) and Chicago. It's not on an industrial scale. It's small-batch roasting, so it's a considerably different business model. Customers will need to offer their time as the brews are handcrafted for them.

Whether a response to the urban coffee cafe culture or a genuine attempt to counter its consumption-first image, I leave it to you to assess. But it is interesting to me that the more we look at doing things automated and machined, the more we see meaning in avoiding their promised efficiencies. For example, Philz Coffee, an American coffee company and coffeehouse chain based in San Francisco, California, is known for its pour-over brews and has no plans to install machines. Its CEO, Jacob Jaber, is focusing on the human elements of slow-craft brews. "In a world of automation and speed," he says, "there need to be things we can do to slow people down and just be present." Increasingly, people are looking for "curated for me." A made-by-humans-for-humans offering. They have the internet for abundance.

Business literature is replete with arguments that herald flawless delivery and praises constant striving for perfection as key tenets of customer retention and overall success. But is it true that a credible customer experience means convenience and seamless delivery? That may be appropriate for interactions that require a low emotional involvement, say a money transfer, or downloading

15 The nine principles of Counterintuitivity

an app. However, brands wanting a higher emotional involvement from their user may want to consider incorporating friction as an integral, intentional part of their humanied customer experience.

It is about both removing and adding friction, and what it offers for a brand—not so much what it makes the product look like. Nothing you produce or do in this world is static. It is not supposed to be. **Things can and should evolve**, and sometimes, something you finalize right now by putting it out into the world won't be completely done. Perhaps that is a good thing; put something out there that is not complete so that the future can remain a little more unpredictable.

Our technologies are not only changing what we do, they are changing who we are. As designers, our responsibility is to **know how our innovations affect human interactions**. We can either continue to focus on only the iteration of the known, exemplified by lovely design execution and an emphasis on engagement, or we can evolve and explore the possibilities to create new meaning and change behaviors for the good of us all. The purpose of focusing beyond what is to be iterated is to empower ourselves to solve complex interconnected systemic problems that are in need of solving.

PART 4 • CREATING MEANINGFUL INNOVATION

chapter 16
Creating Meaning Is A Design Task

DURING WORLD WAR II, Abraham Wald[79], a Hungarian mathematician, was asked to estimate where allied airplanes would benefit from additional armor to prevent them from being shot down. The conventional, predictable wisdom of the time was to look at where returning airplanes had the most the bullet holes; the wings and fuselage. This type of thinking was limited; it was based only on the returning aircraft, not the ones that were lost. Wald introduced a counterintuitive[80], and branded controversial, idea: he recommended that airplanes should see additional armor where there had been the least amount of bullet holes: the engines. This went against all other recommendations from engineers and air combat minds of that day. Wald's stance was that clearly multiple hits to the wings and fuselage could be survived. Numerous hits to the engines could not. His counterintuitive, and labeled unnecessary, thinking delivered more allied survival in the air, some-

---
[79] Profile https://en.wikipedia.org/wiki/Abraham_Wald
[80] https://thenewsrep.com/102000/a-mathematicians-war-how-abraham-wald-helped-win-world-war-ii-without-ever-firing-a-shot/

16 Creating meaning is a design task

thing desperately needed in this war of attrition. Innovation doesn't always mean inventing something new or doing only the obviously needed. It doesn't always happen by doing what seems necessary. Sometimes it is achieved by looking at things from a slightly different angle. Considering the opposite of the typical, almost self-evident solution. **Innovators don't see different things; they see things differently.**

Our innovations often emerge on an axis between economic and technology drivers. Rooted in a company's processes, these dimensions of business and technology are anchored in a company's processes and strategies and usually come together quickly and deliberately. These are variables that already coexist in most enterprises. Hence, we see most innovation processes are driven by technological breakthroughs that are then marketed, or vice versa, with decision-makers initiating innovation efforts based on economic considerations. The focus is on technological feasibility and the marketability of innovations. However, we can only speak of meaningful innovation when the human context is brought into the spotlight; when we make people with their needs, behaviors and attitudes an equal dimension in the innovation process, from creation to delivery, alongside technology and business. Since only humans can attribute "meaning" to things, meaning can only be created through their inclusion in this process. The challenge in this respect is the following: Innovation with technology and business models is already complicated; but when the human factor is added, it becomes complex. Complex requirements between business and technology turn into complex problems that have to be approached with new ways of thinking and working. New ways of thinking and working are the kind of tasks that a design mind loves to tackle. This is good news for our innate human capabilities to design and imag-

Counterintuitivity · making meaningful innovation

ine. If we can embrace the proposition that today is merely a beta for tomorrow.

I have lived and worked in Asia for all of the 21st century. My go-to quip is that Asia, and in particular regions like China and Korea, is half a world ahead of everyone else when it comes to digital and technology. It's a claim that is backed by witnessing leapfrog innovators redefine possibilities, acting out of a single view, not bound by legacy or heritage, or former tech systems that could hold them back. Fearlessly creating new expressions, new experiences, new meanings. Observing and attempting understanding what these mavericks do differently, and looking at what the western societies are labeling as meaningful, it appears to me that a lot of what they are doing successfully is counterintuitive to what we are led to believe is the path to innovation. It's these habits, as well as some of my own, that are the catalyst for this chapter—indeed for the book.

How can we look ahead and imagine what people will value and find meaningful? The only way to do that is to involve people—working together with others. Only a vision of the future that is based on many different views has a chance of being attractive and meaningful to many people. Possibly even whole segments of society. Imagineering such a future needs a well-articulated vision about tomorrow's possibilities, based on an understanding of the systems involved; the human, social, political, cultural, and yes, the technical. It's no longer about business units, but human competencies. We still tend to see corporations as institutions. Ivory towers on barren lands. Instead, can we start seeing them as portfolios of human competencies which can be grouped together, combined and modeled in new, perhaps counterintuitive manners? Let's not limit our view to products only, but needs and purposes. We need to stop thinking in terms of traditional product and services where the

16 Creating meaning is a design task

functionality and acquisition metrics are determining value. What emotions can our interaction enhance, negate, or evoke at that moment in time of human engagement? Can we start asking more naive questions and hope for the impossible? I have gotten more alignment, trust, and momentum by asking "Why can't it be done differently?" than by repeatedly asking "How can it be done better?" In most scenarios, I have found that when I or others ask a question starting with "How," we are jumping to outcomes and solutions, and shut the door on why-not.

Everything we do in the name of innovation and design should be grounded around a central philosophy that today's experience with the world is a combination of physical, digital, and human. Each is a distinct space that is immediate, immersive, and tactile. We have ways to go to make them approachable, kind, and empathetic. The humanness of each is a meaningful story where people either instinctively feel part of, or want to continue being part of, as soon as they come across it. It requires our innovation to be genuine, authentic, and kind, and those are the ingredients we need to use from the very beginning of the innovation processes.

I say all this as someone who loves to work on innovation projects, I love designing for them, shaping their visions, imagining their possibilities. I've learned how ideas work, and more importantly, how they work for brands and people. And that the more we see things in silos, sporadically and inconsistent, the more we reinforce the pattern of thought that nothing much of anything can change. My principles of Counterintuitivity offer a glimpse of why everything you and I have learned and applied on innovation previously is now obsolete and wrong. And if not wrong, it is certainly falling short of potential. The rules of old do not apply, and increasingly,

Counterintuitivity · making meaningful innovation

even for the iterative work, the former principles are running out of steam.

In the world of innovation, it seems we still hold on to the 'build it and they will come' notion. Just put something out there, in the real world, for people to discover, use, and then ultimately love. Sadly, that is not the case, and perhaps it really never was. Humans are now spoiled by choice, awash in a world that is inundated with choices and ideas. More ideas, however, is not better. It's just more. **Counterintuivity is needed**; go full turn, 180 degrees, in the other direction. An uncomfortable act. Especially for those among us who hold onto the belief that we-designers, or we-innovators, are at the center of everything and everyone. It is my ambition that with this book, and its principles, those who have that view are less sure of their answers, investigate their logic a bit more, and step outside their pattern recognition bubble.

The future of innovation is not sales, and not even service. It is meaning. And meaning is found in emotions. Not just 'an experience,' which is an overused and rather lazy metric for 'made you sit up straight for a bit.' There are eight core human emotions that make up the story arc of meaning; enjoyment, surprise, fear, anger, anticipation, sadness, trust, disgust. Everything that makes us, us. Emotions run deeper than disruption and using predictability will prevent us from architecting them. Every innovation needs to locate its core emotion and offer a rollercoaster ride with it. Earlier in the book, I mentioned how our own human contributions are beginning to appear unreliable, clumsy, and wasteful. How we are slaves to our emotions. But our very weakness is also our strength. Despite our most ambitious efforts to demystify them, emotions remain elusive. They are better felt than explained, better portrayed than analyzed. Emotions are raw, they are illogic, irrational, yet they are

16 Creating meaning is a design task

never good or bad. They just are. We don't understand them unless we feel them, and feeling them, of course, is the very blind spot that may prevent us from ever 'objectively' understanding them or writing algorithms for them.

I want to dispel that the only innovation worth pursuing is technological innovation because that is like reducing all innovation to a single concept. Imagine what you would miss out on if you reduced an orchestra to a single violin. Regardless of what gets innovated; meaningful ideas have things in common: they are authentic, imperfect, untested, and they combine a human need with an ambition to transform experience. Genuine innovative ideas focus on the people and societies, with the desire to improve, increase, or radically impact everyday life, with an outcome that is experienced as meaningful.

Looking back at history, we know that the future needs innovation. There are no mistakes in design, there is only the process of learning how to approach the practice, and discovering what to let go of, and what actions are needed next. That journey is unique for each project, and unique for each of its participants. As we design, we may well set out with certain expectations. Wanting the experience or end outcome to be a certain way. But we must keep in mind that the actual experience outcome is not the most important part of the project. We can't control how people react, behave, or interpret the design we put out there. Of course, we will make the effort to match our experience and expertise as to narrow that gap between what people will likely adopt and embrace as a design expression. Yet there are no guarantees that will match our expectations.

The cresting wave of technology—in particular sensors, the internet of things and artificial intelligence—is turning every business into an information business. Big Data will be exponentially bigger, and this will rapidly change business environments, and how we are to leverage technology to decode that data. But it shouldn't only be done under the tyranny of profit and efficiency. Because meaningful change is going to happen: traditional industry boundaries will be blurred, competition will rewrite its rules and so will partnerships. Competing and collaborating will happen within and between dynamic ecosystems, clusters of departments that form evolving partnerships. Systems that are not perfectly controllable and prone to evolve and adapt to changing needs. This means we need to be able to question the meaning of it all, become more than practice-oriented, and use different methodologies to see innovation co-evolve with these new evolving ecosystems.

There is no definite playbook for that, because there shouldn't always be one. Orchestrating meaning in an evolving world will see our innovation practice race ahead of the theory. Which, in itself, is the essence of being innovative. Those who can pioneer new ways to propose more meaningful possibilities will have warranted the reputation of being innovators.

It is why I ask you all to consider more **Counterintuitivity** and the imperfections that should come with creating things of meaning. Our fingerprints are all over what we design, and what we design is our legacy in the world. We are currently at risk of funneling our society down a very narrow path, to a future where we only seek operational excellence and efficiency. Living in **a mono-culture of predictability** (fig9).

As practitioners in innovation, our job is to help create a future that is, by definition, uncertain. If we're only thinking about the short term, the repeatable, the known and familiar, then we are not

16 Creating meaning is a design task

asking questions about the future. We will fall short of our potential because we're not inspiring the world to move to **a multi-culture of possibility** (fig9). We can save the innovation practice from becoming overly predictable. In the shadows of artificial intelligence and machine learning, we must acquire more knowledge and understanding of human sentiments. Because if we don't, we might end up living in societies that no longer have any appreciation whatsoever for the unnecessary, the authentic, the incomplete and definitely not for the ugly. It's easy to hide behind the narrative that the world is simply too big, and too complex, and that the actions of one to bring about change are naïvely futile. Yet change comes from individuals, together.

fig.9 Building a mono-culture of predictability, or building a multi-culture of possibility

So be audacious; consider *doing the seemingly unnecessary, make the ordinary unknown, choose more boredom, create moments of affinity, be authentically ugly, fearlessly moving ahead without regretting decisions, and remain incomplete and unfinished.* And do all this out of conviction and not authority. These are not only the qualities of designing meaningfully, these are inherently human characteristics. And these are also the qualities of what we call home. And as we disrupt, and are disrupted, the least we can do is to ensure that we still feel at home in our profession, and that we use our profession to create that feeling for everyone else.

Counterintuitivity · making meaningful innovation

PART 4 • CREATING MEANINGFUL INNOVATION

chapter 17
The Gift, Now Given

HERE IS WHERE the "exit through the gift shop" sign comes in view—this is the last page of the book. Thank you for being with me. Writing a book is harder than I thought, yet more rewarding than I could have ever imagined. I'm eternally grateful for the opportunity, and for the attention you, dear reader, have brought to it. This is not a theory, or an ideology, or anything of the sort. It's a story—from one personal, fallible point of view.

"*Write what you know.*" Which appeared to me as solid advice. However, composing this book, I found myself resisting that advice. First, I won't lie, because I thought I knew everything on this topic, and could therefore write about it. That resulted in me not writing much of anything. The backlash of that common advice to "write what you know." Why would I not see this as an opportunity to explore new subjects, different connections and rational, unknown topics? If I am making it my soapbox for us all to be more creative and open-minded, be fearless, incomplete and unfinished, then why would I write inside the box I already think I know? Writing this

16 The gift, now given

book, I used what I know as a starting point. It became an opportunity for me to push myself to learn more. About the topics I share, sure, but also about the process of writing. Writing these pages has shown me my learning edge.

But I won't declare that I already understand my argument inside and out. There is no ambition to offer authority here, yet I do hope I respond to a genuine industry crisis with dignity and respect. I wanted this to be a gift to my readers even if you are second-guessing the assumptions and perspectives I offer. Reading, as static as it may portray itself to be, is an interactive activity. To get the most out of something non-fiction, you have to go into the mind of the writer and try to assimilate their thinking patterns in your own mind. The words on the page themselves are secondary to that. It's the dance they create that matters—the context in which they are meant to be understood. It means that words in this book can't be looked at as static. I want them to be dynamic.

So yes, I write about what I know, but I did not stop there. I expand on what I do know. It's a subtle nuance. The more I tackled this topic of meaning in the pursuit of innovation, the more I uncovered that I held myself an incomplete picture of an issue that is larger and even more translucent than I imagined. My book, its content, and what it evokes in you and me, is imperfect. I think that is okay. Perfection to one person differs to the next. It differs in one single person from morning to evening as each of us feels our expectations alter and morph. All I want to obtain is a flavor of imperfection, but with an aim for precision. The precision of an objective; to start more conversations with more interesting people and save innovation from its pitfalls. That would, in my eyes, be good news for all of us. Planet included.

Counterintuitivity · making meaningful innovation

Innovating or designing without a deeper sense of meaning will have us become reactive and territorial. Making the multiple disciplines that are involved in the process retreat into craft silos, chasing proxy metrics only. We need to embrace the fact that products and their features are temporary. Today's design solution is tomorrow's problem to solve. When we set out to innovate, discussion of value and intent are to be supplemented by conversations around the meaning of it all. Meaning will outlive the usefulness or novelty of a feature. Practitioners can amplify meaning in the creation of innovative proposals by frequently integrating that which is deemed meaningful. When all is discussed, designed, and delivered, the thing we innovated should reflect a deep understanding of the context, the environment, and the human that experiences both. That is always the constant. How we address this will always change as more possibilities emerge from new tech. It is meaning, however, that has stood the test of time.

Increasingly, people are finding gratification and a sense of purpose through creating connections, memories, and experiences. People are looking deeper for a sense of identity that can't be derived only from material product purchases. People want to feel as if they are involved in something bigger than themselves. They want to be able to identify with the products and services they use. People want to feel like their lives have meaning. What is meaning? Meaning is what gives us a sense of importance or worth. It's very specific to each of us and it helps us interpret the world and decide how to act. Meaning is what helps us assess and determine what we value, believe, and desire. Every choice that we make in our lives contributes to our own personal framework of meaning. Innovation isn't just about making things frictionless, or just about usability, or even just delight. It is about taking products from being usable to delightful, and then beyond that—to meaningful. Design is a way for us to

16 The gift, now given

deliver deep meaning to our customers through the experiences we craft. We must strive to elevate the value we deliver to our customers from a basic, functional one, to one that goes much beyond. Design needs to not only deliver pleasure and delight, but must deliver the deep meaning that we know people are seeking. Counterintuitive thinking and different ways of working can enable deeper connections, deeper meaning to meaningful experiences. The palette of meaning is rich and diverse; accomplishment, beauty, community, creation, duty, enlightenment, freedom, harmony, justice, oneness, redemption, security, truth, validation, wonder. All are core human meanings that offer many more possibilities beyond function, efficiency, and predictability.

Some of you may have found depth and truth here. There will be those who see me as a "mile wide and an inch deep" kind of messenger. To both, I say delve even deeper into your niche, look and find new angles to research, play your own devil's advocate and take a stance you usually wouldn't. Become students of life and share the learning. Start with what you know, then expand on what you do know. Talk outside your circles, go present or lecture, or manifest your views in writing; whatever the shape or form of your journey, it is therapeutic. And courageous; I applaud you. This book is now part of my journey, and it revealed that, for me, writing is therapy. What a novel idea. That pun wasn't intended, but let's roll with it.

Counterintuitivity · making meaningful innovation

Acknowledgements

FINALLY AN ACKNOWLEDGEMENT. If this book proves to be of use, I would want to dedicate it to my colleagues, friends, clients and peers, past, present and future. You were, are or will be part of this continued journey of mine, and my interactions with you all continue to shape me and educate me in ways that are still emerging.

Then there are those of you who have played a larger role in having me write, offering encouragements, instructions and support. I know you know who you are, now I would like more people to know it too. None of this would have happened without Ziqq Ratiff planting that seed for me to consider writing all this. Nor would I have arrived at having my story in physical and e-form without the guidance of Scott Allen, whose book guidance and coaching helped me ride the rollercoaster. Shoutout to Qat Wanders, Dee Turner and Allison Goddard; I learned so much from each of you. I am deeply grateful to Khai Seng; you are my learning edge and fellow wave length surfer.

Thank you for your endorsement; Jorge Arango, Jean Lin, and Chris Jones. To Michael Cina; your art viscerally captures the soul of this book - you keep inspiring me.

Speaking of support, attention and time! Thank you for journeying with me: Jess, Amy, Matt, Davar, Adam, Darren, Stephen, Ray, Tom Yee, Val, Daylon, Alex, Susan, Murali, Maik, John, Caitlyn, Kiat, James R, James F, Rob, Tom, Mo, Kenneth, Erin, Dan, Tim, Kyani, Sam, Cyrille, Philip, Paul, Steve, David, Samatha, Remy, and Edo.

My deepest gratitude to my wife, Konnie and my son, Kaeden. Our family time is precious, and feels like a never-enough thing, and yet you both gave me the space to complete this work — I am deeply grateful for your generosity, love and belief.

References

Nothing can be created out of nothing
(Lucretius, 94–55 BC: De Rerum Natura)

Ahmed, S., Wallace, K. M., & Blessing, L. T. M. (2003). Understanding the differences between how novice and experienced designers approach design tasks. Research in Engineering Design.

Alexander, C. (1964). Notes on the synthesis of form. Cambridge, MA: Harvard University Press.

Arango, Jose (2018). Living in Information - Responsible Design for Digital Places. Rosenfeld press.

Bartneck, C. (2007). Design methodology is not design science. Proceedings of the CHI 2007 Conference on Human Factors in Computer Systems. New York: ACM.

Battistella, C., Biotto, G., & De Toni, A. F. (2012). From design driven innovation to meaning strategy. Management Decisions, 50, 718–743.

Benedek, M., Jauk, E., Fink, A., Koschutnig, K., Reishofer, G., Ebner, F., & Neubauer, A. C. (2014). To create or to recall? Neural mechanisms underlying the generation of creative new ideas. NeuroImage, 88, 125–133.

Bilda, Z., & Gero, J. S. (2007). The impact of working memory limitations on the design process during conceptualization. Design Studies.

Bonnardel, N., & Marmèche, E. (2004). Evocation processes by novice and expert designers: Towards stimulating analogical thinking. Creativity and Innovation Management, 13(3), 176–186.

Brandon Klein, Dan Newman (2016) Facilitating Collaboration - notes on facilitation for experienced collaborators. The Value Web.

Brown, T. (2009). Change by design: How design thinking transforms organizations and inspires innovation. New York, NY: Harper Business.

Carlgren, L. 2013. Design thinking as an enabler of innovation: Exploring the concept and its relation to building innovation capabilities. Göteborg, Sweden: Chalmers University of Technology.

Cross, N. (2011). Design thinking: Understanding how designers think and work. Oxford, UK: Berg.

Dong, A. 2015. Design × innovation: Perspective or evidence-based practices. International Journal of Design Creativity and Innovation 3 (3): 148–163.

Esslinger, Hartmut (2012) Design Forward, creative strategies for sustainable change. Arnoldsche Art Publishers.

Fraser, H. (2012). Design works: How to tackle your toughest innovation challenges through business design. Toronto: Rotman/UTP Publishing, University of Toronto Press.

Flaherty, James (2998) Coaching - evoking excellence in others, 3rd edition (2010). Routledge Taylor & Francis Group.

Holmes, Kat (2018). Mismatch, how inclusion shapes design. The MIT press.

Kalogerakis, K., Lüthje, C., & Herstatt, C. (2010). Developing innovations based on analogies: experience from design and engineering consultants. Journal of Product Innovation Management.

Kerne, A., Smith, S. M., Koh, E., Choi, H., & Graeber, R. (2008). An experimental method for measuring the emergence of new ideas in information discovery. International Journal of Human–Computer Interaction

Kim, J., Bouchard, C., & Ryu, H. (2012). Emotion finds a way to users from designers: Assessing product images to convey designer's emotion. Journal of Design Research,

Kim, J., Ryu, H., & Kim, H. A. (2013). To be biased or not to be: Choosing between design fixation and design intentionality. Proceedings of the CHI 2013 Conference on Human Factors in Computer Systems. New York: ACM.

Kimbell, L. 2011. Rethinking design thinking: Part 1. Design and Culture 3 (3): 285–306.

Kosslyn M., Stephen and Miller G. Wayne (2013, 2015) Top brain, bottom brain. Harnessing the power of the four cognitive modes. Simon and Shuster Paperbacks.

Lawson, B. (1997). How designers think: The design process demystified (3rd ed.). Oxford, UK: Architectural Press.

Lawson, B. (2005). How designers think: The design process demystified. Boston, MA: Architectural Press.

Lawson, B., & Dorst, K. (2009). Design expertise. New York, NY: Architectural Press.
Löwgren, J., & Stolterman, E. (2004). Thoughtful interaction design: A design perspective on information technology. Cambridge, MA: MIT Press.

References

Liedtka, J. (2014.) Innovative ways companies are using design thinking. Strategy & Leadership 42 (2): 40–45.

Martin, R. (2009). The design of business: Why design thinking is the next competitive advantage. Boston, MA: Harvard Business School Press.

Moggridge, B. 2007. Designing interactions, Cambridge, MA: MIT Press.
Price, R., C. Wrigley, and K. Straker (2015). Not just what they want, but why they want it: Traditional market research to deep customer insights. Qualitative Market Research: An International Journal 18 (2): 230–248.

Rittel, H. W. J., & Webber, M. M. (1974). Wicked problems. Man-made Futures, pp. 272–280.

Schön, D. A. (1983). The reflective practitioner: How professionals think in action. New York, NY: Basic Books.

Schwarz, N. (2010). Meaning in context: Metacognitive experiences. In B. Mesquita, L. F. Barrett, & E. R. Smith (Eds.), The mind in context (pp. 105–125). New York, NY: Guilford.

Scott, Susan (2017). Fierce Conversations, acheiving success at work & in life. Berkley US, Piatkus UK.

Shaw, C. (2007). The DNA of customer experience: How emotions drive value. New York: Palgrave Macmillan.

Shaughnessy, Adrian (2005). How to be a graphic designer, without losing your soul. Princeton Architectural Press. New York.

Sigman, Mariano (2015). The secret life of the mind, how our brain thinks feels and decides. William Collins 2017.

Simon, H. 1969. The sciences of the artificial. Cambridge, MA: MIT Press.

Sloman, Steven and Fernbach, Philip. (2017). The Knowledge Illusion - why we never think alone. Riverhead Books, an imprint of Penguin Random House.

Tomico, O., Winthagen, V. O., & van Hesit, M. M. G. (2012). Designing for, with or within: 1st, 2nd, and 3rd person points of view on designing for system. Proceedings of the Nordic Conference on Human-Computer Interaction. New York: ACM.

Turner, Raymond (2013), Design leadership, securing the strategic value of design. Gower Publishing Ltd, UK.

Tseng, M. M. and Piller, F. T. 2003. The customer centric enterprise: advances in mass customization and personalization, Berlin: Springer.

Verganti, R. (2009). Design-driven innovation: Changing the rules of competition by radically innovating what things mean. Boston, MA: Harvard Business Press.

Von Hippel, E. 2005. Democratizing innovation, Cambridge, MA: MIT Press.

Wrigley, C., & Straker, K. (2016). Designing innovative business models with a framework that promotes experimentation. Strategy and Leadership.

Author's Bio

The Skinny

MARIO VAN DER MEULEN. Designer. Strategist. Speaker. Author. *Graphicdesignosaurus*.

Formerly as creative director at Frog, and currently as a Principal Designer at Foolproof, Mario Van der Meulen discovers, designs and delivers experience design principles. He is an ambidextrous designer/strategist with over 25 years of international experience, based in Singapore. He brings an exceptional ability and passion for the intersection of product, service, brand and strategy design. He contributes to the measurable success of agency operations and the impact of consumer-facing products and services at scale. With a proven ability to develop meaningful experiences for users and brands - to the benefit of both. In 2010, CBS Weekly recognised Mario as "One of Fifty Innovation Design Pioneers in China". In 2018, one of his Foolproof projects received the 2018 IDC Smart City Asia Pacific Awards (SCAPA).

In our design-by-humans-for-humans world, he works to dispel the misconceptions about how breakthrough ideas for meaningful innovation are made. Then shape the now, near and next. By offering range, from product-centric to a systems view, he helps people come together, work together, create together and change the world. Driven by the belief that people ignore design that ignores people, he leads a process where each participant can find the right conversation, the right advice, the right mind-meld, at the right time for the right reasons. To win in today's climate, corporations need short-term wins and long-term growth. Mario helps brands do it by cultivating decision intelligence, by providing expertise in insights, strategy, trends, foresight and creativity. Outfitting brands to excel in current culture—and in the rapidly unfolding future.

The design Mario cares most about is humanity, and how we can craft thoughtful, empathetic acts of design to bring people closer to the meaningful, the purpose-led. Doing so will see technology work on human terms, and create a future that looks and feels more human by tech, not less because of it. An avid keynote speaker, workshop facilitator and an author on Creativity, Change and Design Mindset, he has delivered over 150 speeches and creative sessions in over 20 countries on 4 continents.

To find out more, be inspired in the areas of creativity, change or design mindset, or if you are interested in connecting with him to book a speech or workshop (now or in the future) follow Mario here or check out these resources:

mvdm.me
mvdmpublishing.com
linkedin.com/in/mariovdm
twitter.com/MarioVDMeulen
instagram.com/oiramnavred/